AF596798

A LETTING GO

A Journey of Rediscovery

AMITESH MANI TIWARI

INDIA · SINGAPORE · MALAYSIA

ISBN

Hardcase 979-8-89673-843-5
Paperback 979-8-89673-491-8

Contents

Acknowledgments

First and foremost, my deepest gratitude goes to my family—my pillar of strength and inspiration. This journey, this dream, and this story are all deeply rooted in the values you have instilled in me.

To my late grandfather, **Shri Pandit Madan Mohan Tiwari**, this novel is a tribute to your immense love and the cherished childhood memories shaped by your stories. Your wisdom and belief in me continue to inspire and guide me. Though you are no longer here, your blessings remain my strength. With all my love and gratitude, this story is for you.

To my **Papa ji (Mr. Indramani Tiwari)** and **Maa (Mrs. Sanyogeeta Tiwari)**, your unwavering belief in me has been my greatest motivation. Your sacrifices, love, and guidance have laid the foundation for every achievement in my life. You are my greatest blessings, and this story is for you and because of you.

To my brother, **Aditya Mani Tiwari**, who has stood by me through every storm, encouraged me to rise during my darkest days, and is one of the main reasons this story came to life—thank you for your love, support, and belief in me. Without you, this dream would still be just a thought.

This story wouldn't have been possible without the memories and bonds of college life. Some of the best moments in this novel were inspired by the friendships I shared during those days. A special thanks to **Shubham Singh**, who was not just my friend but a constant source of encouragement. From brainstorming chapters to cheering me on when I doubted myself, Shubham, you were there every step of the way. To **Abhishek Kumar Sahu** and **Abhinval Pal**, you've been my comrades in laughter, struggles, and dreams. The late-night talks, endless debates, and shared experiences from our college days played a huge role in shaping this story.

I also want to acknowledge my close friends who feel like family—**Satyendra Mishra** and **Satyam**. You've always stood by me, offering unconditional support and encouragement. Whether it was through your words of wisdom or just being there during my moments of doubt, you've been a constant source of strength and positivity. Thank you for believing in me even when I didn't.

Amitesh Mani Tiwari ✍

Prologue

Why should you read this story? Because it's not just a story—it's a mirror. It reflects the lives of countless students across campuses, navigating the chaotic blend of aspirations, expectations, and heartbreaks. It's about the sleepless nights spent worrying over placements, the unspoken pressures of being "good enough," and the quiet struggles that often go unnoticed.

I began writing this story in **March 2024**, drawing from the memories, emotions, and lessons of my college years. It's a tapestry woven from moments shared with friends, the laughter echoing in dorm rooms, the tearful goodbyes, and the unspoken camaraderie that grows in late-night conversations. It's not just a story about Ankit; in many ways, it's about my friend, about me, and perhaps even about you.

This story is for anyone who's ever felt lost in a crowded lecture hall, overwhelmed by assignments, or unsure of their place in a world that moves too fast. It's for those who've sought solace in shared dreams, found meaning in small victories, and faced heartbreaks that left them questioning everything.

It's especially for the young men who carry the weight of expectations in silence, striving for excellence while grappling with self-doubt. For those who've been told to "man up" when their hearts ached, and for anyone who has ever wondered if they'd ever be truly understood.

This is **Ankit's story**. But in so many ways, it's yours too.

Ankit was the boy everyone thought had it all—sharp, ambitious, and a natural leader. But beneath the surface, he struggled with insecurities, the crushing weight of being the "perfect student," and a deep yearning to be seen and loved for who he truly was.

He fell for Anishka, a girl who seemed like everything he wasn't—confident, free-spirited, and effortlessly radiant. In her, he saw a spark of hope, a vision of something beyond his rigid world. But love, as he discovered, is rarely simple. For Ankit, it became a mirror reflecting his deepest fears and vulnerabilities.

This is a story of heartbreak and resilience. It's about how Ankit lost himself in the pursuit of love, only to find his way back through the ashes of pain. It's about finding strength in letting go, embracing failure as a teacher, and rediscovering oneself amidst the chaos.

It's a story of healing through creativity, finding peace in ancient wisdom, and learning the quiet power of detachment. Ankit's journey reminds us that success isn't just about placements or achievements—it's about becoming someone you're proud of, despite the scars life leaves behind.

This story isn't just for students; it's for anyone who has faced heartbreak, self-doubt, or the pressure to fit into someone else's mold. It's for those searching for meaning in the messiness of life.

So, step into Ankit's world. Walk with him through love, failure, and rediscovery. His journey isn't just his own—it's a guide for anyone who's ever wondered, **Will I be okay?**

1. This novel could resonate with and help several types of people:
2. **People Facing Emotional Abuse:** Those experiencing emotional or mental abuse in relationships, whether romantic or otherwise, can find comfort in seeing a protagonist who struggles with similar pain but eventually overcomes it.
3. **Young Men in Emotional Turmoil:** The story could help young men who feel misunderstood or disrespected in relationships, guiding them through emotional healing, building resilience, and finding strength.
4. **People Struggling with Letting Go:** Individuals who are stuck in toxic relationships but fear leaving due to emotional attachment may find inspiration in how the protagonist navigates these challenges and learns to let go.
5. **Those Seeking Personal Growth:** Readers interested in self-discovery, personal transformation, and the healing process will

connect with the themes of rebuilding self-worth and emotional freedom.

6. **People Who Use Creativity to Heal:** Creative individuals who cope with emotional struggles by turning to their imagination, art, or generosity will see themselves in the protagonist's journey.
7. **Empathetic Readers Wanting Insight:** Those who want to better understand the emotional challenges and struggles men face in modern relationships could gain valuable perspective from this novel.

PART 1

THE SPARK OF CONNECTION

Chapter 1

Collision of Worlds

The early morning sun streamed through the tall trees lining the campus pathways, casting golden patches of light onto the dew-covered ground. A soft breeze carried the faint scent of grass, and the occasional chirp of a bird added a sense of calm to the quiet morning. It was the kind of moment that could make even a final-year engineering student forget about deadlines and the looming stress of placements—if only for a while.

Ankit stretched in bed, blinking as the sunlight peeked through his thin curtains. He was usually the kind of person who welcomed routine—wake up, study, and head out for the day. But today, something felt different. His thoughts were tangled, his mind unable to shake off the lingering impact of last evening's guest lecture.

He sat up, glancing around his small but organized room. His desk was stacked with coding books, notebooks, and a laptop, all strategically placed. A calendar on the wall had red circles marking placement deadlines and project submissions. Normally, the sight of that calendar was enough to kickstart his day with focus. Today, though, his thoughts kept drifting back.

The lecture wasn't anything extraordinary on the surface—another talk about artificial intelligence. But the way it had been delivered stuck with him. The speaker, Anishka, wasn't a professor or industry expert but a final-year student like him. She had stood on the stage with quiet confidence, explaining complex concepts with simplicity and passion. It wasn't just her technical depth that captivated him; it was the way she made everything feel bigger—like their work could genuinely change the world.

Ankit shook his head, trying to push the thought aside. He walked over to the small shrine in the corner of his room, lighting the diya in front of the idols of Lord Krishna and Lord Hanuman. The warm glow flickered, and he closed his eyes, saying his daily prayer for clarity and strength. But even as he prayed, his mind kept returning to the same question: Why had her words stayed with him so much?

The buzz of his phone interrupted the quiet moment. It was a message from Ravi, his best friend.

"Bro, meet me at the mess at 10 A.M. Hot parathas and chai today—don't miss it!"

Ankit smiled, shaking his head. Ravi's enthusiasm for food was unmatched, even for something as ordinary as parathas. Ravi, with his round face and ever-present grin, had a way of making even the dullest mornings lively. He was the opposite of Shubham, their other close friend—Shubham was quieter, more methodical, always scribbling ideas in his notebook. Together, the three of them balanced each other out, surviving the chaos of engineering life.

Grabbing his bag, Ankit headed out. The campus was already alive with activity. Groups of students strolled across the pathways, some heading to the library, others chatting under the sprawling banyan tree near the main building. The hum of laughter and chatter filled the air, blending seamlessly with the rustling leaves.

When Ankit reached the mess hall, the familiar smell of freshly made parathas and masala chai greeted him. Ravi waved enthusiastically from a corner table, where he was already halfway through his plate. Next to him, Shubham was sipping his chai, notebook open as always.

"Look who finally showed up," Ravi teased as Ankit slid into a seat beside him. "What, did your algorithms hold you hostage this morning?"

"Or maybe something else is on his mind," Shubham added with a sly grin, not looking up from his notes.

Ankit raised an eyebrow. "I don't know what you're talking about."

Shubham chuckled. "Really? Because you've been weirdly quiet since last night's lecture."

Ravi's curiosity was instantly piqued. "Oh, the AI lecture? What's the story?"

"There's no story," Ankit said, grabbing a paratha to avoid their prying eyes. "It was just... different."

Ravi leaned in, smirking. "Different how? The topic or the speaker?"

Ankit shot him a look. "The topic, obviously."

Shubham exchanged a knowing glance with Ravi, but they let it go for now. "Well, whatever it was, you'd better keep that inspiration alive. The placement season's not waiting for anyone," Shubham said, returning to his notebook.

They ate in comfortable silence after that, the occasional joke from Ravi breaking the stillness. But even as Ankit joined in their banter, his mind wandered. He couldn't help but replay moments from the lecture—the way Anishka had spoken about AI not just as a tool but as a responsibility.

"Technology is a reflection of its creators," she had said, her voice steady yet passionate. **"It's not just about building something—it's about asking why you're building it in the first place."**

That line had struck a nerve. Ankit loved coding, but he rarely thought about the "why." His projects were impressive on paper, sure, but they often felt mechanical, detached. For the first time, he wondered if he was missing something—something deeper.

"Earth to Ankit," Ravi said, snapping his fingers in front of his face. "You've been staring at that paratha like it holds the secrets of the universe."

Ankit laughed, shaking off his thoughts. "Just thinking about the guest lecture this afternoon," he lied.

"Good," Shubham said. "You need to snap out of whatever trance you're in. We've got a lot to prepare for."

As they finished their breakfast, Ravi cracked another joke, and Shubham muttered something sarcastic in reply. But Ankit stayed quiet, lost in thought. The questions stirred by Anishka's words wouldn't leave him alone, and he couldn't shake the feeling that this was the start of something he didn't fully understand yet.

As they walked out of the mess hall, the sun was higher in the sky, casting sharp shadows across the campus. The day felt unusually alive, as if something big was just around the corner. And for the first time in a long while, Ankit found himself looking forward to the unknown.

"Sometimes, the most significant changes begin with a simple question—a spark that turns the ordinary into something extraordinary."

Chapter 2

Cracks in the Shield

The day was clear, but Ankit's thoughts were anything but. The morning class dragged on, the monotony of equations and graphs failing to capture his attention. Usually, he was the type to sit upright, pen poised, catching every word his professor said. Today, though, his notebook lay open but untouched, the pages starkly empty.

The classroom hummed with low activity—pens scratching against paper, the soft murmur of whispered conversations, and the faint whir of the overhead fan. Ankit sat in the back, his arms folded, his gaze distant. The professor's voice faded into the background as his mind drifted elsewhere.

He leaned back in his chair, his thoughts returning to the previous evening.

"It is my pleasure to introduce today's speaker," the anchor had announced, their voice brimming with enthusiasm. "A brilliant mind already shaping the future of artificial intelligence—Anishka Rao."

The name hadn't stood out to him at first. Guest lectures were a dime a dozen, and he had walked into the hall expecting yet another dry talk filled with technical jargon. But then she had walked onto the stage, and something had shifted.

Anishka Rao was striking, not in an intimidating way, but in how she carried herself. Her presence seemed to light up the room, her sharp features softened by an easy smile. Her long black hair was pulled back into a neat ponytail, and she wore a simple yet elegant kurti that complemented her confident yet approachable demeanor. But it was her eyes that caught Ankit's attention the most—bright and focused, like she saw the world with a clarity he couldn't quite understand.

The hall, noisy moments before, had fallen into a hushed silence as she began speaking. Ankit remembered the way her voice carried—not loud, but firm and steady, with a warmth that drew everyone in.

"AI is not just the future," she had said, her tone purposeful, "it's the present. The way we interact with it now will define how we solve problems tomorrow. My work at IIT Patna has shown me that AI isn't just about data—it's about the people who need it the most."

Her words were more than just technical explanations; they were a call to action. She had shared examples from her research—AI models designed to assist rural farmers in predicting crop yields, systems aimed at improving healthcare access in underserved areas.

For the first time, Ankit had seen AI as more than lines of code. It wasn't just about algorithms or neural networks—it was about its impact on real lives.

"Bro, you're in another world again," Shubham's voice interrupted, pulling him back to the present. Shubham sat beside him, nudging his elbow. "You're not even pretending to take notes anymore. What's up?"

Ankit blinked, momentarily disoriented. "Nothing. Just... thinking."

"Thinking about Anishka?" Shubham teased, his grin widening. "That talk must've really made an impression, huh?"

Ankit shrugged, trying to play it cool. "It was a good lecture. That's all."

Shubham wasn't buying it. "You should've seen yourself yesterday. I don't think you blinked the entire time she was on stage."

Ravi, sitting in front of them, turned around, catching the tail end of the conversation. "Wait, what? Ankit, the human algorithm, got distracted by something that wasn't code? Now, this I have to hear."

Ankit shot him a warning look, but Ravi was already grinning. "So, what's the plan? You gonna go talk to her or just sit here daydreaming?"

"Talk to her? Are you insane?" Ankit scoffed. "She's... way out of my league."

"Oh, come on," Shubham said, rolling his eyes. "You can't keep hiding behind that excuse."

"It's not an excuse," Ankit muttered, feeling heat creep up his neck. "She's brilliant, okay? And she's doing things I can't even imagine. Why would she waste her time on someone like me?"

Shubham sighed, leaning back in his chair. "You're hopeless, man. But whatever. Just don't spend the whole day staring into space."

The bell rang, signaling the end of the class. Students began packing their bags, the sound of zippers and shuffling feet filling the room. Ankit shoved his notebook into his bag, though he hadn't written a single word. As they stepped out into the bright afternoon sun, Shubham nudged him again.

"You know, if you're so interested, you could at least find her on LinkedIn or something."

"I'm not a stalker," Ankit shot back, but there was a hint of a smile on his face.

Ravi laughed, throwing an arm around Ankit's shoulder. "Relax, bro. We're just saying—it wouldn't hurt to step out of your comfort zone once in a while."

As they walked across the bustling campus, Ankit found his mind wandering back to the lecture. He remembered the way Anishka had responded to a professor's question with the same calm confidence she had shown throughout the talk. Even when challenged on the technical aspects of her research, she had answered with precision, her passion shining through.

There was something about her that unsettled Ankit in the best way. She made him question the way he saw the world—his narrow focus on grades, projects, and job offers. For the first time, he wondered if he had been limiting himself, missing out on the bigger picture.

"Ankit, you coming?" Ravi called out, jolting him from his thoughts. They were heading toward the canteen for their usual post-class chai, but Ankit paused.

"Actually, I think I'll catch up with you guys later," he said.

Shubham raised an eyebrow. "Don't tell me you're planning to—"

"I just need some time to think," Ankit interrupted, cutting him off.

His friends shrugged and walked on, leaving Ankit alone. He wandered aimlessly for a while, eventually finding himself near the auditorium where the lecture had taken place. The stage was empty now, the echoes of Anishka's voice replaced by silence.

Ankit sat down on one of the empty benches, staring at the stage. He wasn't sure what he was looking for, but he felt a strange pull, as though the questions stirring inside him could only be answered here.

For the first time in a long time, he didn't feel certain about his path. And maybe, he thought, that was okay.

"Sometimes, the cracks in our shield aren't weaknesses—they're openings for something new to come through."

Chapter 3

Hidden Shadows

The sun hung lazily in the sky, casting long shadows across the courtyard as Ankit and Ravi strolled toward the hostel after another mind-numbing lecture. Shubham trailed behind, eyes glued to his phone, muttering something about an incomplete assignment. The warm afternoon breeze swirled around them, carrying the faint chatter of students and the clatter of the mess hall nearby.

Ravi broke the silence with a loud snort. "Man, remember first year?" he asked, grinning at Ankit. "When Shubham looked like he wanted to punch you the moment you walked into class?"

Ankit smirked, grateful for the distraction. "How could I forget? I was so confused."

Ravi laughed, nearly doubling over. "You were confused? I was scared. Shubham had that death glare going on—like you stole his favorite pen or something."

Shubham, catching up, rolled his eyes. "I wasn't *that* bad."

"Not that bad?" Ravi teased, raising an eyebrow. "You literally told me, 'I can't sit near that guy. He looks just like Kunal.' Or was it Krunal? Whatever your ex's husband's name was."

Shubham groaned, running a hand through his hair. "Yeah, okay. Fine. I was a little... irritated."

"'Irritated'?" Ravi said, eyes wide. "Bro, you hated him."

"Can you blame me?" Shubham said, throwing his hands up. "It was my first day back after finding out my ex got married. Then this guy walks in looking like Kunal's long-lost twin. It felt like fate was mocking me."

Ankit chuckled. "So I was guilty by resemblance?"

"Pretty much," Shubham admitted, grinning. "But hey, look at us now. I don't even think about that idiot anymore."

"Well, it's good to know I'm more than just a face to you now," Ankit said, shaking his head with a laugh.

The easy banter lightened the mood, but Ankit's thoughts soon drifted back to her. Anishka. He hadn't spoken to her since the lecture, but the memory of her words—and the way she carried herself—lingered in his mind. She had this way of commanding attention, of drawing people in without even trying. But there was something else, too. Something he couldn't quite put into words.

The teasing continued as they reached the hostel, but Ankit's responses grew shorter. Shubham noticed first.

"Hey, you good?" he asked, nudging Ankit. "You've been zoning out a lot lately."

"Yeah, just... thinking about that presentation," Ankit said, trying to sound casual.

Shubham smirked. "Oh, you mean the one by *Anishka*?"

"Shut up," Ankit muttered, though the heat rising in his neck betrayed him.

"Come on," Ravi chimed in, slinging an arm around Ankit's shoulders. "You've been weird ever since that talk. Just admit it—you're into her."

"It's not like that," Ankit said quickly. "I just... I don't know. She's interesting."

Ravi let out a dramatic sigh. "Bro, you sound like a rom-com cliché."

"Yeah," Shubham added, grinning. "Next thing you know, you'll be writing poetry about neural networks."

Ankit rolled his eyes, but he couldn't deny there was some truth to their teasing. Something about Anishka had unsettled him—not in a bad way, but in a way that made him question things he'd never really thought about before. It wasn't just admiration for her intelligence or confidence. It was the way she seemed to view the world differently, like she saw possibilities he hadn't considered.

Days passed, and Ankit's thoughts of Anishka didn't fade. He found himself scanning the crowd during lectures and lingering on campus longer than usual, hoping for a glimpse of her. But it wasn't until a week later that their paths finally crossed.

It was late in the evening, and Ankit was leaving the library, his bag slung over one shoulder. The campus was quiet, the usual buzz of activity replaced by the soft rustle of leaves and the hum of streetlights. He was halfway across the courtyard when he spotted her.

Anishka was sitting alone on a bench, her face illuminated by the soft glow of her phone. The dim light from the nearby lamp cast long shadows across her features, giving her an almost ethereal quality. Ankit hesitated, his heart racing. He could keep walking, pretend he hadn't seen her. Or he could go over and introduce himself.

Before he could decide, she looked up and met his gaze. There was no turning back now.

"Hey," he said awkwardly, stopping a few feet away. "Anishka, right? I, uh... saw your presentation last week. It was really impressive."

She smiled, but it was small, almost guarded. "Thanks," she said, her voice calm but distant.

Ankit shifted his weight, suddenly unsure of himself. "I mean, the way you talked about AI—it wasn't just technical. It felt... personal. Like you actually cared about the impact."

Her eyes flickered with something—surprise, maybe?—but it was gone as quickly as it appeared. "That's the point, isn't it?" she said. "Technology isn't just about what we can do. It's about what we *should* do."

Ankit nodded, trying to keep the conversation going. "Exactly. I've never really thought about it like that before. You made it feel... bigger than just algorithms."

For a moment, Anishka's expression softened. "Most people don't think about it that way. They're too focused on the mechanics to see the bigger picture."

There was a pause, and Ankit hesitated, wondering if he should say more. But before he could, Anishka glanced at her phone and stood up. "Anyway, I should get going. It was nice talking to you."

"You too," Ankit said, stepping aside as she walked past. "Maybe I'll see you around?"

"Maybe," she replied, her tone unreadable.

As she disappeared into the shadows, Ankit stood there, his thoughts swirling. The conversation had been brief, but it had left him with more questions than answers. There was something about her—something just beneath the surface—that he couldn't quite figure out.

Over the next few weeks, Ankit and Anishka crossed paths more often. They weren't exactly friends, but there was an unspoken connection between them, a pull that neither seemed willing to acknowledge. On the surface, everything seemed fine. Anishka was friendly and engaging, her intelligence and passion shining through in every interaction. But there were moments when her warmth faded, replaced by a cool detachment that left Ankit feeling uneasy.

It wasn't obvious, not at first. But the more time they spent together, the more Ankit noticed the cracks. A hesitation in her smile, a flicker of doubt in her eyes—small things, but enough to make him wonder.

One evening, after another brief conversation with Anishka, Ankit found himself sitting in the common area with Shubham and Ravi. They were talking about assignments and weekend plans, but Ankit was only half-listening.

"You've been weird lately," Shubham said, nudging him. "What's going on with you?"

Ankit hesitated. "It's... complicated," he said finally.

"Is this about Anishka?" Ravi asked, raising an eyebrow.

Ankit didn't answer, but his silence was enough.

"You like her," Shubham said, his tone serious for once. "Just... be careful, okay? She's hard to read."

Ankit nodded slowly, the unease in his chest growing. Something about Anishka didn't quite add up. But for now, he didn't have the answers.

"Sometimes, the shadows we ignore are the ones that end up consuming us."

PART 2

THE PULL OF DEPENDENCY

Chapter 4

The Illusion of Closeness

The unease about Anishka lingered in the corners of Ankit's mind, like a faint whisper he couldn't quite catch. He tried to shake it off as he prepared for the day ahead. Today was Krishna Janmashtami—a day that always brought him clarity, a pause in the chaos of his life. He needed that now more than ever.

The golden morning sunlight seeped through his curtains, bathing his small room in a warm glow. The scent of incense wafted through the air, mixing with the faint aroma of sandalwood from the diya flickering in his shrine. Ankit adjusted the small idols of Lord Krishna and Lord Hanuman, his movements slow and deliberate. For him, Krishna was more than a deity—he was a silent companion in moments of doubt, a reminder to trust in the greater plan.

As Ankit whispered his prayers, his voice low and steady, his thoughts wandered. The words he spoke carried more weight this morning, as though he hoped Krishna might answer the questions swirling in his mind.

"What am I doing? Why can't I stop thinking about her?"

His chest tightened at the thought of Anishka, but he pushed it aside. This wasn't the time.

"Krishna," he murmured, bowing his head. "Help me see the truth. Show me the right path."

The buzz of his phone pulled him out of the quiet moment. He glanced at the screen: a message from Shubham.

"Bro, meet me after your pooja. Got some stuff to tell you!"

A faint smile tugged at Ankit's lips. Shubham always respected his rituals, never interrupting his Janmashtami prayers. Ankit replied with a quick thumbs-up, his fingers moving instinctively, and turned back to the shrine. As the flame flickered in the diya, he felt a momentary calm wash over him, as if Krishna himself had whispered, **"Trust yourself."**

The campus buzzed with activity as Ankit stepped out of the hostel later that day. Groups of students strolled along the main pathways, their laughter and chatter filling the air. Somewhere in the distance, the rhythmic beats of dhols announced the preparations for the evening's Janmashtami celebrations.

Shubham caught up with him near the canteen, his grin as wide as ever. "Done with your pooja?" he asked, falling into step beside Ankit.

"Yeah," Ankit said, nodding. "What's this 'stuff' you had to tell me?"

Shubham leaned in, lowering his voice like he was about to share a state secret. "Anishka's best friend just got back on campus. Apparently, they're inseparable."

"Her best friend?" Ankit asked, feigning casual interest, though his heartbeat quickened.

"Yeah, some girl named Priya," Shubham said, waving it off. "Thought you'd want to know, seeing as you've been, you know... a little preoccupied."

Ankit smirked, shaking his head. "You're imagining things."

Shubham raised an eyebrow but let it go. "Sure, sure. Just don't let it mess with you."

Over the next few days, Ankit noticed Anishka more than ever. She always seemed to be just within reach—walking past him in the library, laughing with Priya in the canteen, or catching his eye during a lecture. Their conversations were brief, almost inconsequential, but they carried a weight that kept pulling him in.

"Hey," she'd say with a smile that lingered just a little too long. "Thanks for helping me with that assignment. I couldn't have done it without you."

"It's no big deal," Ankit would reply, his voice steady even as his heart raced. "Happy to help."

The praise felt intoxicating, like a warmth that settled in his chest. But there were moments, fleeting but sharp, when her demeanor shifted. A missed text from him would be met with a cold edge in her voice the next day. A moment of distraction during their conversations would earn him a questioning glance, as if to say, **"Aren't I worth your full attention?"**

Ankit told himself it was nothing. She was just being... herself. But the doubt crept in, slow and insidious.

One evening, as Ankit sat at his desk, his phone buzzed with a message from Anishka.

"I'm at the library. Can you help me with something?"

His chest tightened, the familiar mix of anticipation and unease swirling inside him. Without a second thought, he grabbed his bag and headed out. The campus was quiet under the evening sky, the dim glow of streetlights casting long shadows across the pathways. Somewhere in the distance, a faint melody played—a haunting, romantic tune that mirrored the turmoil in his mind.

When he reached the library, Anishka greeted him with her usual warmth, her smile soft but dazzling. Priya sat beside her, flipping through a book, but it was clear who commanded the room. Anishka had a way of drawing people in, of making you feel like you were the only person who mattered.

"Thanks for coming," she said, her voice smooth, almost melodic.

"It's no problem," Ankit replied, settling into the chair beside her. "What do you need help with?"

They worked together for a while, their heads bent over notes and textbooks. Every so often, her hand would brush against his, sending a spark up his arm. Her praise came in soft murmurs, barely audible but deeply felt.

"You're amazing at this," she whispered once, her eyes meeting his. "I wish I had your patience."

Ankit felt his cheeks flush. "It's nothing, really."

Priya, watching the subtle dance between them, eventually stood up with a teasing smile. "I'll leave you two to... figure things out."

Ankit chuckled nervously, but his focus was already back on Anishka. The moments that followed were quiet, charged with unspoken words. She leaned closer as they worked, her perfume filling the small space between them. For a brief moment, Ankit let himself believe that this connection was real, that he wasn't imagining the bond he felt growing between them.

But as the evening wore on, the cracks began to show. Anishka's warmth would falter—just for a second, but enough to leave Ankit questioning himself. When they finished, she turned to him, her smile faint but polite.

"You didn't have to do all this for me," she said, her tone light but pointed. "I don't need anyone to take care of me."

The words hit harder than he expected. "I just wanted to help," he said, his voice quieter now.

"I know," she replied, her gaze unreadable. "But you don't have to, Ankit. I'm fine on my own."

As she walked away, her figure disappearing into the dim light of the library exit, Ankit felt a hollowness settle in his chest. Her words replayed in his mind, each one cutting deeper than the last. Had he overstepped? Misread her intentions? The unease from earlier grew heavier, wrapping around him like a suffocating fog.

Back in his room, Ankit stared at his phone, her message still glowing on the screen. His chest felt tight, his thoughts a tangled mess of doubt and longing. The diya in his shrine flickered faintly, its light offering little comfort now.

"Sometimes, the line between love and illusion is so thin that you don't notice you've crossed it until you're already lost," he thought, his throat tightening with the weight of the realization.

Anishka's shadow loomed larger than ever in his mind, and for the first time, he wondered if he was in too deep—if the connection he felt was real, or just an illusion he'd built around her.

Chapter 5

Slipping Into Shadows

The sun was high in the sky, its warmth cutting through the cool morning breeze. It was a perfect Sunday, and Ankit couldn't help but feel a lightness in his chest as he walked with Shubham and Ravi. The campus was quieter than usual, with most students using the day off to sleep in or catch up on assignments, but for Ankit, it felt like the perfect day for something spontaneous.

The plan was simple—lunch with Anishka, a casual hangout to shake off the week's stress. Ankit had spent the morning replaying their recent interactions in his head. Lately, their conversations had felt different, like there was a subtle shift in their dynamic. He wasn't sure what it meant, but he couldn't deny the growing hope inside him.

Shubham, ever the joker, was already talking about food. "If you're taking Anishka out today, I hope you've got good taste, man," he teased. "Girls like that expect fancy places, not your Chole Bhature obsession."

Ravi laughed, slapping Ankit on the back. "He's right! You can't impress her with oily street food and extra bhature."

Ankit grinned, playing along. "You guys underestimate the power of Chole Bhature. It's not just food; it's an experience. Besides, she loved it the last time."

"Ah, yes," Shubham mused, stroking an imaginary beard. "A girl who loves Chole Bhature. Hold onto her."

Their laughter echoed through the courtyard, but Ankit's thoughts drifted to Anishka. He was looking forward to their lunch, hoping the day would bring them closer. Yet, beneath his excitement, there was a flicker of doubt he couldn't quite place.

As the hours passed, Ankit received a message from Anishka: **"Hey, I'll be a little late. Something came up. Let's meet around 2?"**

He frowned slightly but brushed it off. Delays happened. **"No problem,"** he replied, trying to keep things casual.

By 2 PM, Ankit was at their usual spot—the Chole Bhature stall. The air was warm, the smell of fried bhature wafting through the small crowd. He checked his phone again. Nothing.

Ten minutes later, his phone buzzed, and relief washed over him—until he read the message: **"Hey, something's come up with an old friend. Can we reschedule? Sorry about this."**

An old friend? Ankit hesitated, the words sinking in. She hadn't mentioned anyone visiting. Before he could overthink, another message appeared: **"I promise we'll meet up soon. Just dealing with some stuff."**

He typed a quick response: **"No worries. Catch you later."** But the tightness in his chest didn't ease.

Anishka sat at the edge of her bed, phone in hand, staring at Ankit's reply. Her thumb hovered over the screen, tempted to send another message, but she stopped herself. She placed the phone face down and leaned back against the wall, letting out a sigh.

From the other side of the room, Priya spoke up. "You canceled again, didn't you?"

Anishka groaned, running a hand through her hair. "I didn't cancel. I postponed."

"Same difference," Priya replied, folding her arms. "What's your deal with him anyway? He's clearly into you."

"It's not that simple," Anishka said quietly, avoiding Priya's gaze. "Ankit's... nice. He's sweet. But it's a lot."

"A lot?" Priya raised an eyebrow. "The guy worships you. How is that a problem?"

Anishka looked down, her voice soft. "That's exactly the problem. I feel like I'm leading him on, and I don't know how to stop."

Priya sighed, sitting down beside her. "So, what's really going on? Is it about Akash?"

Anishka stiffened at the name but didn't reply. Priya continued, her tone gentler now. "You can't keep holding onto him, Anishka. It's been over for months. And Ankit... he's not Akash."

"I know that," Anishka said, her voice barely above a whisper. "But every time I try to let someone in, it feels... wrong. Like I'm betraying something. Or someone."

Priya shook her head. "You're not betraying anyone. You're just stuck in your own head. If you don't figure this out, you'll end up hurting both yourself and Ankit."

Anishka nodded slowly but didn't respond. She reached for her phone, her fingers brushing the screen before pulling away. She couldn't bring herself to say what she really felt—not to Priya, not to Ankit, not even to herself.

Back in his room, Ankit replayed the day's events in his mind. Shubham's voice echoed in his ears: **"Maybe she's keeping her options open."**

The thought made his stomach churn. Was he just another name on her list? He wanted to believe their connection was real, but every interaction left him more confused.

The next day, Ankit spotted Anishka on campus, talking to a guy he didn't recognize. They stood close, their conversation animated. For a moment, Ankit froze, the sight stirring something sharp and bitter inside him. He tried to walk past without looking, but Anishka caught his eye and waved. Her smile was warm, but it didn't reach her eyes.

"Hey," she called out, her tone casual. "Missed you yesterday."

Ankit forced a smile. "Yeah, no problem. Hope everything's okay."

"Yeah, just... hectic," she said, brushing her hair back. "Catch you later?"

Before he could respond, she turned back to the guy, her attention already elsewhere. Ankit walked away, his chest tight with a mix of jealousy and doubt.

That night, Ankit sat alone in the common area, staring at his phone. He wanted to message her, to ask what was going on, but he couldn't bring himself to do it. What if Shubham was right? What if he was more invested than she was?

He opened their chat, his fingers hovering over the keyboard. A dozen unsent messages filled his mind, each one tinged with frustration, confusion, and longing. Finally, he closed the app, tossing his phone onto the table.

"Sometimes, the shadows we fall into are of our own making, born from the illusions we cling to, hoping they'll become something real."

Ankit leaned back, his gaze fixed on the ceiling. The shadows around him felt heavier than ever, and for the first time, he began to wonder if he'd ever find his way out.

Chapter 6

Heart on a Tightrope

The quiet rustle of paper filled the exam hall, broken only by the relentless ticking of the clock. Ankit stared at his unit test paper, the questions blurring before his eyes. Normally, he'd breeze through a test like this, his mind sharp, his answers precise. But today, the numbers felt like strangers, the algorithms foreign. His pencil hovered uselessly over the first question.

The invigilator's footsteps echoed through the silent hall, each step a cruel reminder of the time slipping away. Ankit glanced at the clock, the hands ticking louder with every second. He gripped his pencil tighter, willing himself to focus, but his thoughts betrayed him, spiraling back to Anishka.

It had been days since they'd properly talked, and the space between them felt wider than ever. One moment she was warm, her laughter lighting up his world; the next, she was distant, her messages short and cryptic. And then there was the phone screen—a name he didn't recognize flashing in that brief moment when her phone buzzed during their last conversation.

"Focus," he muttered under his breath, but the paper remained a blur. The sinking feeling in his chest deepened. By the time the invigilator collected the papers, Ankit knew he'd bombed it.

Back at the hostel, the corridor buzzed with life. Groups of students lounged against the walls, discussing the exam, cracking jokes, or planning a trip to the chai stall. Someone had propped open their door, blasting Bollywood songs that echoed through the hall. Ankit walked past them all, their chatter barely registering.

His room was a sanctuary of chaos—textbooks stacked precariously on the desk, stray wrappers from late-night snacks littering the floor, and a half-empty water bottle rolling under his bed. He dropped his bag and collapsed into the chair, his mind too heavy to think.

A knock on the door pulled him from his thoughts. Shubham leaned in, a Parle-G biscuit hanging from his mouth, and two steaming cups of chai balanced in his hands.

"Dude," Shubham said, plopping down on the bed. "You look like someone stole your notes. What happened?"

Ankit sighed, running a hand through his hair. "Flunked the test."

"Flunked?" Shubham raised an eyebrow, passing him a cup of chai. "That's not you, man. You don't flunk."

"I do now," Ankit muttered, the bitterness in his voice surprising even himself.

Shubham studied him for a moment before taking a sip of chai. "This is about Anishka, isn't it?"

Ankit didn't respond immediately, the silence answering for him. Shubham sighed, setting his cup down. "You've been off, man. Always distracted. You barely play cricket anymore, you miss the chai breaks at Sahu's stall, and now this? Whatever's going on, it's screwing with you."

"It's complicated," Ankit admitted, staring at the chipped rim of his cup. "She's... I don't know. One day, she's all in. The next, she's pulling away. And now..." He hesitated, the words catching in his throat. "Now, I don't even know where we stand."

"Bro," Shubham said, leaning forward. "You're walking a tightrope, and it's all in your head. She's either into you, or she's not. But you can't keep letting her mess with your focus."

Ankit wanted to argue, but he couldn't. Shubham wasn't wrong. His life had been a mess of late-night assignments, canceled cricket matches, and missed chai breaks—all because he couldn't stop chasing the idea of something more with Anishka.

That evening, Ankit sat at his desk, his textbook open but untouched. His phone buzzed, the glow of the screen pulling his attention. It was a message from Anishka:

"You didn't have to help me with all that, you know. I can handle things on my own."

Ankit read the message twice, his chest tightening. He thought back to the hours he'd spent helping her with her project, convinced he was doing the right thing. But now, her words felt like a slap, a dismissal of everything he'd done. He typed a reply, paused, then erased it. What could he say that wouldn't make things worse?

The next day, Ankit wandered through campus, his mind heavy. Near the cricket field, a group of students cheered as someone hit a six, the echo of the ball cracking against the bat ringing through the air. A vendor pushed his chai cart past the library, calling out, "Garam chai! Samosa!" The familiar rhythm of college life continued around him, but Ankit felt like an outsider, trapped in his own storm.

Then he saw her—Anishka—near the library steps. She was talking to a guy Ankit didn't recognize, their conversation animated. She laughed, the sound light and effortless, and for a moment, Ankit felt invisible.

As he walked past, she noticed him. "Hey!" she called out, waving. Her smile was warm, but her eyes held something distant.

"Hey," Ankit replied, forcing a smile. "Everything okay?"

"Yeah, just busy," she said, brushing a strand of hair behind her ear. "We'll catch up soon?"

"Sure," Ankit said, but his voice lacked conviction. As she turned back to her conversation, he walked away, the familiar weight settling in his chest.

That night, Ankit lay in bed, staring at the ceiling. Shubham's words echoed in his mind: **"She's either into you, or she's not."**

The tightrope he had been walking felt thinner than ever, swaying dangerously beneath his feet. He thought about his test, the missed cricket matches, the chai breaks he no longer enjoyed. He thought about Anishka's smile, so close yet so far. And he thought about the message she had sent, short and sharp, cutting through his hope like a blade.

"Sometimes, the line between love and illusion blurs so much that we don't realize we're slipping until it's too late."

As Ankit drifted into an uneasy sleep, one thought lingered: something had to change. And soon.

Chapter 7

When It All Falls Apart

Outside Ankit's window, the hum of hostel life carried on—animated discussions about the upcoming cultural fest mingled with the sound of someone practicing a slightly off-key rendition of "Kabira" on a guitar. The corridor smelled faintly of Maggi and detergent, and the occasional burst of laughter drifted in, a reminder of the life Ankit had once been immersed in but now felt painfully detached from.

At his desk, Ankit stared at his unit test paper, the red marks glaring back at him like open wounds. His hands rested limply on either side of the paper, his fingers curling slightly, as though they might crumple it. He couldn't bring himself to touch it again. The numbers and formulas that once made sense to him now seemed like a language he'd forgotten. He ran a hand over his face, his palm damp with the sweat that clung to his temples.

The door creaked open, and Shubham and Ravi strolled in, their voices loud and full of energy. Ravi waved a crumpled pamphlet like a victory flag, while Shubham trailed behind with his usual air of quiet skepticism.

"I'm telling you, yaar, this debate competition is our chance to shine!" Ravi exclaimed, dropping onto Ankit's bed with a bounce. "Free Maggi for participants. What more motivation do you need?"

Shubham snorted, tossing his phone onto the table. "You? A debate? Ravi, you couldn't win an argument even if the other person didn't show up."

"It's not about winning," Ravi said dramatically, clutching the pamphlet to his chest. "It's about the free food. Priorities, my friend."

Ankit couldn't help the faint smile that tugged at his lips. Ravi's antics never failed to lighten the mood, but today, even that couldn't pull him out of the fog enveloping his mind.

Shubham caught sight of the paper on Ankit's desk and leaned over to take a closer look. His eyebrows shot up. "Wait, what? Ankit. Fail?" He held the paper up like it was evidence in a court case. "Dude, you never fail."

Ravi peered over Shubham's shoulder, his grin widening. "Whoa. Ankit failing a test? That's like Shah Rukh Khan starring in a horror movie—it just doesn't happen! What gives, man?"

Ankit leaned back in his chair, pressing his fingers into the edge of the desk. He tried to laugh it off, but the sound that escaped his throat was hollow. "I've just... been distracted."

Shubham exchanged a look with Ravi, one of those silent conversations only close friends could have.

"Distracted, huh?" Shubham said, his tone deliberate. "Let me guess—this has something to do with a certain AI genius named Anishka?"

Ravi clapped his hands together as if he'd just solved a great mystery. "Of course! It all makes sense now. Bro, you've been off your game ever since that lecture. She's in your head, rent-free."

Ankit forced a smile, shaking his head. "It's not that," he said, though even he wasn't convinced by his own words.

"Sure, sure," Ravi teased. "Except you've been walking around like a zombie, staring at your phone every five minutes, and now you're failing tests. Classic case of—what do they call it?—unrequited love syndrome."

Shubham nudged Ravi with his elbow. "Knock it off, man. He's already beating himself up. You don't need to pile on."

The room fell quiet for a moment, the only sound the faint strumming of the guitar from the corridor. Ankit stared at the edge of his desk, his fingers brushing against the wood grain. He wanted to say something, anything, to explain how he felt. But the words wouldn't come.

Ravi broke the silence, his voice softer now. "Hey, man. We're just messing with you. You'll figure this out. You always do."

Ankit nodded, but the knot in his chest only tightened.

His phone buzzed in his hand, the vibration sharp against his palm. The name on the screen made his breath hitch—*Ma*.

Shubham glanced at the phone and grinned. "Perfect timing. Maybe your mom can talk some sense into you."

Ankit hesitated, his thumb hovering over the screen. He knew that if he answered, she'd sense something was wrong. But he couldn't ignore her. Taking a deep breath, he stepped out into the hallway.

"Hello, Ma?"

Her voice was warm, a balm he hadn't realized he needed. "Ankit, beta, how are you? You haven't called in so long. Is everything alright?"

He swallowed hard, gripping the phone tighter. "I'm fine, Ma. Just busy with studies."

There was a pause, the kind that only mothers could fill with meaning. "You sound tired, beta. Are you eating properly? Taking care of yourself?"

Ankit closed his eyes, leaning against the cool wall. "I'm fine, Ma. Really."

"Your father paid your hostel fees this week," she said gently, her tone careful.

Ankit's heart sank. "How did he manage that? I thought we were waiting until next month."

She hesitated. "He didn't want to worry you. But... we had to take out a small loan. Against the land in the village."

The air seemed to leave his lungs all at once. "What?" His voice cracked, barely above a whisper. "Why didn't you tell me?"

"We didn't want to burden you, beta," she said, her voice trembling slightly. "Your father said we'd manage. He wanted you to focus on your studies. You're our hope, Ankit."

He felt a tightness in his chest, a knot that seemed to constrict his breathing. The guilt was overwhelming, wrapping around him like a vice. "Ma... I'm sorry. I didn't know."

"There's nothing to be sorry for," she said softly. "Just do your best. That's all we've ever wanted."

The call ended, but her words lingered in his mind, each one a weight pressing down on him. The village land wasn't just property—it was their future. And now, his education had become a burden they couldn't shoulder without sacrificing everything.

Back in his room, the weight of his parents' sacrifices bore down on him. His test paper lay on the desk, a glaring reminder of his failure. His friends watched him quietly, the usual banter replaced with concern.

"You good, bro?" Ravi asked, his voice low.

Ankit nodded, though his throat felt tight. "Yeah. I just... need to figure some things out."

Later that night, when the hostel was quiet and his friends had drifted to sleep, Ankit sat alone. His thoughts churned, a storm of doubt and determination. He knelt before the small mandir in his room, the flickering flame of the diya casting long shadows across his face.

"Krishna," he whispered, his voice raw. "I don't know what to do. Show me the way... please."

The calm that followed wasn't an answer, but it was enough. For the first time in days, his mind stilled. And as he closed his eyes, he made a silent promise: he would rise above this. For his parents. For himself.

"Sometimes, the hardest battle isn't with the world outside—it's with the expectations we carry within."

PART 3

THE BREAKING POINT

Chapter 8

Silent Withdrawal

Ankit sat at his desk, staring at his textbooks, but his mind was elsewhere. It had been days since he last replied to Anishka's messages. Every time her name flashed on his phone, his chest tightened, but he forced himself to ignore it. He had made a promise to himself after that phone call with his mother—he would focus, he would get his grades back on track, and he would let go of this toxic cycle.

But it wasn't that easy. Even though he didn't respond to Anishka, the temptation to check her messages gnawed at him. His phone buzzed again, and he glanced down to see her name. The familiar surge of emotion hit him, but this time, he resisted. He threw the phone face down on his bed and picked up his notebook, trying to immerse himself in his studies.

The silence between them felt suffocating, but Ankit told himself it was for the best. Yet his mind kept wandering back to their past, to the nights when they would talk for hours. He remembered one specific night, a few weeks before everything started to crumble.

It was well past curfew, and both of them were supposed to be asleep. But as usual, Ankit found himself on the terrace, his phone pressed to his ear.

The faint hum of crickets filled the air, mingling with the distant sound of laughter from a nearby hostel. The night sky stretched above him, dotted with stars, but his focus was on the voice on the other end of the call.

"Do you ever wonder if this is all we'll ever be?" Anishka's voice was softer than usual, almost vulnerable.

"What do you mean?" Ankit asked, feeling the familiar flutter in his chest.

"I mean... do you ever think about us? About the future? Or is this just... something for now?" Her words lingered in the silence that followed.

Ankit's heart raced. This was the closest she had ever come to talking about their relationship in real terms. He wanted to say something, anything, but before he could respond, she continued.

"Never mind. I guess I'm just overthinking. I've been doing that a lot lately."

Her words, though casual, left Ankit restless. He had spent months wondering what they were, what they meant to each other, but every time he tried to get closer, she pulled away, leaving him confused and yearning for more.

Ankit snapped back to the present, shaking his head. No, he couldn't keep doing this. He couldn't keep thinking about her, wondering what might have been, obsessing over conversations that led nowhere. He was supposed to be done with this. But even as he tried to focus on the pages in front of him, his mind drifted back to her, to the way she would laugh, to the quiet moments they had shared. Every memory felt like a weight pressing down on him, reminding him of how much she had taken up space in his mind.

But now, things were different. Ankit had started to pull himself back together—at least academically. His last test results had been better than expected. He had managed to stay focused long enough to improve in a few subjects. His professors had even noticed the shift, complimenting him on his progress. And yet, despite these small victories, the internal conflict remained.

Every time he sat down to study, the memories of Anishka crept in. He would see her smile in his mind, hear her voice in his head, and he would be right back to where he started—unsure, conflicted, and emotionally tied to someone who had become more of a distraction than anything else.

Far away, in her room, Anishka sat cross-legged on her bed, scrolling aimlessly through her phone. Her messages to Ankit remained unread, and the silence gnawed at her. She wasn't used to him ignoring her, and it unsettled her more than she cared to admit.

Priya's voice broke the stillness. "Still waiting for him to reply?" she asked, leaning against the doorframe with a knowing smile.

Anishka sighed, setting her phone aside. "I don't know. He's been so distant lately. It's like he's avoiding me."

Priya walked over and sat down beside her. "Maybe he's just trying to focus on his studies. You know how he gets about academics."

"It's not just that," Anishka said, her voice quieter now. "I feel like... I pushed him too much. Or maybe I wasn't clear about what I wanted. I don't know."

Priya studied her for a moment before speaking. "Look, Anishka, you can't keep sending mixed signals and expect him to figure it out. If you care about him, you need to tell him. Otherwise, you're both just going to keep hurting."

Anishka nodded, but the words didn't settle her heart. She didn't know what she wanted—at least, not fully. But she did know one thing: she missed Ankit, and the silence between them felt unbearable.

Ankit threw down his pen in frustration. How could he be so stupid? Why was it so hard to move on? His phone buzzed again, and this time, he couldn't resist. He picked it up, his heart racing as he opened the message.

It was a simple "Hey" from Anishka.

For a moment, he just stared at it. Part of him wanted to respond, to fall back into the old patterns of late-night conversations and shared moments. But another part of him—the part that was growing stronger every day—knew that he couldn't. Not anymore.

Ankit stared at the phone in his hand, the unopened message from Anishka still glowing on the screen. His finger hovered over the screen for what felt like an eternity, torn between the familiar pull of old habits and the silent promise he had made to himself just days ago.

He took a deep breath and set the phone down, untouched. He had made his decision—at least for now. The path ahead was uncertain, and the emotional storm was far from over, but for the first time in a long time, he felt a flicker of clarity.

"Sometimes, to find yourself again, you have to lose everything you thought you needed."

The silence in the room felt heavier now, but also quieter. He wasn't running anymore. He wasn't ignoring the pain, the confusion, or the regret. He was facing it—one step at a time. And with that, he knew that the hardest part wasn't letting go of Anishka; it was letting go of the version of himself he had built around her.

As the first light of dawn crept through the window, Ankit knew that the next step wouldn't be easy. But this time, he would walk forward, not out of desperation, but out of determination.

Chapter 9

Rekindled Moments

The morning started like any other. Ankit found himself in his usual corner of the library, flipping through textbooks with a sense of urgency. The recent unit test results had been a stark reminder of how much he had let things slip, and ever since, he had thrown himself into his studies. The library had become his sanctuary, a place where silence promised focus and isolation. But even there, his mind wandered, replaying memories from the past year, and once again, Anishka found her way into his thoughts.

The library was unusually quiet, the faint hum of the AC the only sound in the background. Rows of books loomed over him, their spines worn and faded, yet they seemed to mock him with their permanence. He had come here seeking focus, but instead, he found himself drowning in his thoughts.

He smirked, recalling one of his favorite moments—how Ravi, in typical fashion, had misread the exam schedule and missed an entire test week, instead spending the weekend binge-watching his favorite series. "Classic Ravi," Ankit mumbled to himself, chuckling at his friend's blunders. He remembered Shubham too, the joker of the group, the self-proclaimed 'King of Nicknames.'

Shubham had a knack for giving everyone in their batch new, often ridiculous names that somehow stuck. His light-heartedness had been the glue that held the group together, even during their most stressful periods.

Yet, no matter how much Ankit tried to immerse himself in these light-hearted memories, a familiar tightening feeling crept into his chest. Anishka. Even though he had ignored her messages for days, even though he told himself he had to focus on his studies, her name lingered in his mind. She was like a constant shadow, always present, no matter how hard he tried to outrun her.

Every day had become a game of avoidance. Ankit had mastered the art of walking the long way around campus, taking back routes and side exits to steer clear of Anishka's usual hangouts. He made sure to time his lunch breaks carefully, checking the campus schedules to avoid crossing paths with her between classes. Despite his best efforts, there were moments he would catch a glimpse of her from afar—smiling, chatting with friends, completely unaware of the turmoil raging inside him. Each time their paths almost crossed, his heart would race, and he would quickly avert his gaze, pretending not to see her. But the knot in his chest only tightened.

At night, Ankit would sit alone on his hostel bed, staring at his phone. Every notification felt like a ticking bomb, and more often than not, it was Anishka. Each message left unread was a weight on his conscience, but still, he resisted. He knew one reply would undo all his progress. It would pull him right back into the storm he was trying so hard to escape. His phone buzzed yet again, and for a split second, he considered opening it. Instead, he threw it face down onto the bed and returned to his textbooks.

"Failure isn't an option," Ankit whispered under his breath, hoping the words would steel his resolve. But no matter how hard he tried to focus, the shadow of Anishka was always there, like a whisper at the back of his mind.

The quiet of the library, though soothing, had become a double-edged sword. It gave him the space he needed to study, but it also left him too much time to think. His mind would wander, replaying conversations he had had with Anishka, thinking about the 'what ifs.' He wondered if he had made the right decision. Had he cut her off too soon? Could they have worked things out if he had just tried harder?

His hand drifted toward his phone, her unread messages glaring back at him. It was a cycle he couldn't escape—study, think about Anishka, feel guilt, repeat. Before he could succumb to the urge to check her messages, the phone rang, startling him out of his thoughts.

An unknown number flashed on the screen. Hesitant but curious, Ankit answered, "Hello?"

There was a pause—a long one. And then, a familiar, shaky breath broke the silence. "Why are you doing this to me?"

The voice was fragile, trembling with emotion. Ankit froze, his heart skipping a beat. He knew that voice anywhere.

"Anishka?"

Her name barely left his lips before she began crying. Her sobs were quiet but filled with an unmistakable hurt. Ankit's chest tightened, guilt flooding him like a tidal wave.

"Why are you ignoring me? Why won't you talk to me?" Her voice cracked between sobs, each word laced with frustration and sadness. "What did I do, Ankit? Why are you pushing me away like this?"

Ankit closed his eyes, guilt washing over him like a tidal wave. He hadn't been ready for this confrontation, hadn't thought this moment would come so soon. The decision to distance himself had seemed logical at the time, but hearing Anishka like this made him question everything.

"It's not like that, Anishka," he said softly, running a hand through his hair. "I just—there's too much going on. My grades, my family, the future—I'm trying to stay focused."

"But you promised me, Ankit," she sobbed. "You said you wouldn't leave me like this."

Her words cut deep—deeper than he had expected. He hadn't meant to hurt her, hadn't realized how much his silence would affect her.

Anishka's sobs quieted for a moment, her voice raw with vulnerability. "Do you even care about me anymore? Or was I just... convenient?"

"That's not true," Ankit said immediately, the words tumbling out before he could stop them. He took a deep breath, trying to steady his voice. "Let's meet. We need to talk. Face to face."

"Where?" Her voice was barely above a whisper, fragile with hope and pain.

"The garden behind the library," he replied, standing up and grabbing his jacket. "Meet me there in ten minutes."

As he hung up, his heart pounded with a mix of anticipation and dread. He didn't know what he would say to her—or if he could even find the words. But deep down, he knew this meeting wouldn't bring the closure he pretended to seek. It would only open wounds neither of them had the courage to face.

"Sometimes, the loudest cries for help come from the silence between two people. And sometimes, all it takes is a single conversation to break the quiet."

Chapter 10

Fleeting Happiness

The evening air was warm, filled with the lingering scent of marigolds from the Ganesh Chaturthi festivities earlier in the day. Students milled around the campus, their faces alight with the joy of celebration, but for Ankit, it felt like a world apart. The sounds of laughter and prayer drifted to him as he walked toward the garden behind the library, his steps weighed down by the confrontation ahead. He couldn't shake the feeling that tonight would change everything.

He paused for a moment at the edge of the dormitory courtyard, where rows of diyas flickered gently along the pathways. Groups of students sat together on the grass, their laughter carrying into the air like echoes of a life Ankit could no longer recognize. It was a night of unity, of shared joy, but inside him, there was only dissonance. Anishka's words on the phone—fragile and full of hurt—had left a crack in the walls he had tried so hard to build.

"You promised me..."

The memory of her voice tugged at him. He thought he had been doing the right thing by stepping away, by avoiding her, but now that decision felt hollow. How could he explain it all to her when he barely understood it himself?

As he approached the garden, he saw her sitting on the bench under the neem tree. The glow of a nearby streetlamp illuminated her silhouette. Her posture was tense, her hands fidgeting with the edge of her scarf, and her face was partially hidden behind her hair. Even from a distance, Ankit could sense the storm brewing inside her. His heart ached with guilt as he walked closer, every step dragging him through the weight of their shared history.

The wait felt endless. Anishka sat on the cold wooden bench, her mind swirling with questions and doubts that refused to settle. She had spent hours replaying their last few conversations—or rather, the lack of them—searching for some sign, some clue of what had gone wrong.

What had she done to push him away? Was it something she said? Something she didn't say?

The festive air around her felt suffocating, the laughter of her peers a painful reminder of the happiness that seemed just out of reach. She glanced down at her phone, scrolling through the unread messages she had sent to Ankit over the past few weeks. Each one was a plea wrapped in casual words. Each one had been met with silence.

The silence had been the hardest part—the uncertainty, the waiting, the loneliness. Anishka had always prided herself on being independent, on not needing validation from anyone. But with Ankit, it had been different. He had become her anchor in ways she hadn't even realized until he was gone.

Her thoughts were interrupted when she saw him approaching. For a brief moment, a flicker of relief passed through her—he had come. But as their eyes met, the weight of the past weeks crashed over her again. She stood up quickly, brushing her scarf over her shoulders as if trying to compose herself. She wasn't sure what to expect from this meeting, but she knew one thing: she needed answers.

Ankit stopped a few feet away, unsure of what to say. The silence between them felt louder than the faint hum of Ganesh Chaturthi prayers in the distance. Finally, Anishka broke it, her voice trembling but firm.

"Why, Ankit?" she began, her eyes glistening with unshed tears. "Why did you just... disappear? Why didn't you talk to me? I thought we were closer than this. I thought we were... something more."

Her words hit him like a punch to the gut. He looked down at the ground, his hands stuffed into his pockets. "I needed space," he said softly. "Everything was getting too... complicated. My grades were falling, my family needs me to stay focused, and I just couldn't handle everything at once."

"Complicated?" Anishka's voice rose, her frustration spilling over. "Do you think my life isn't complicated? Do you think I don't have my own struggles? But I still tried to be there for you, Ankit. I still thought we had each other." Her voice cracked, and she looked away, biting her lip to keep the tears at bay.

Ankit took a step closer, his heart twisting at the sight of her pain. "It wasn't about you," he said, his voice thick with regret. "It's not that you did anything wrong. It's just... I couldn't find the balance anymore. Everything was falling apart."

Anishka shook her head, her emotions tumbling out in a flood. "Then why didn't you tell me? Why did you shut me out like I didn't matter? Do you have any idea how that made me feel?"

He wanted to answer, to explain the storm inside him, but the words wouldn't come. How could he tell her that she mattered too much, that his feelings for her had become overwhelming? That he had been afraid of losing himself in the intensity of their connection?

"I'm sorry," he said finally, his voice barely audible. "I didn't mean to hurt you, Anishka. I just... I didn't know how else to deal with everything."

Her expression softened slightly, but the hurt lingered. "You think saying sorry fixes everything?" she asked, her voice quieter now. "You think it erases the weeks I spent wondering what I did wrong, waiting for a reply that never came?"

Ankit looked down, shame burning in his chest. "No," he admitted. "It doesn't fix anything. But it's the truth. I messed up, and I'm sorry."

The silence between them stretched on, heavy with unspoken words. Anishka turned away, staring at the ground as she tried to gather her thoughts. When she finally spoke, her voice was softer but still tinged with sadness.

"I don't know if I can forgive you for this," she said. "I don't know if things will ever be the same between us."

Ankit felt his heart sink, but he nodded. "Maybe not," he said quietly. "But I still care about you, Anishka. I always will. I just... I need time to figure things out."

Anishka nodded, her shoulders slumping in defeat. "I understand," she said. "But you need to understand something too, Ankit. You can't keep running away from your feelings. You can't just shut people out when things get hard."

Her words lingered in the air like an unspoken challenge. Ankit knew she was right. He had been running—running from his emotions, from the confusion and chaos that had taken over his life. But maybe it was time to stop.

"Thank you for meeting me," Anishka said finally, her voice barely above a whisper. "I needed to hear this from you, even if it hurts."

"I'm sorry," he repeated, his voice full of regret.

As they stood there in the fading light, the echoes of the festival drifting in the distance, Ankit couldn't help but feel that something had shifted between them. The bond they had shared—whatever it had been—had changed. Maybe it wasn't broken, but it was different now. And as they parted ways, walking in opposite directions, Ankit realized that fleeting happiness could be just as painful as losing it.

"Sometimes, happiness is as fleeting as the moments that create it. But even in those moments, we learn something about ourselves—about who we are and what we truly want."

PART 4

UNRAVELING THE BOND

Chapter 11

Echoes of Contentment

It was 11:30 AM, and the sun hung high in the sky, casting long, golden shadows across the bustling campus. Students poured out of their first classes of the day, the pathways alive with chatter, laughter, and the occasional shuffle of hurried footsteps. For Ankit, the energy around him felt like a gentle hum in the background—a rhythm he was moving to but not entirely in sync with.

The sprawling campus was its own world, a maze of ancient trees, wide-open fields, and familiar gathering spots. The canteen buzzed with life, a sanctuary of chai-fueled conversations and the enticing aroma of fresh samosas. Today, Ankit wasn't rushing to his next lecture. For once, he had allowed himself a break, choosing to soak in the fleeting calm before the chaos of final-year responsibilities returned.

Walking toward the cafeteria with Ravi and Shubham, he couldn't help but smile as their banter filled the air.

"Another lecture, another day wasted trying to decipher that professor," Shubham groaned, throwing his hands up dramatically. "Does he even know what he's saying, or is it all a test to see how much nonsense we can endure?"

"Maybe if you stopped daydreaming, you'd understand a thing or two," Ravi quipped, smirking.

Ankit chuckled, only half-engaged in their conversation. His thoughts were elsewhere, drifting to Anishka as they often did. Despite his attempts to focus on his studies, her name lingered at the edge of his mind like an unsaid thought. Their dynamic was an undefined space, a fragile balance between friendship and something more. Lately, though, he had started questioning how much longer he could live in this ambiguity.

As they reached the cafeteria, the boys claimed a table by the window overlooking the lush campus gardens. Ankit's phone buzzed, and his heart leapt when he saw Anishka's name light up the screen. *Where are you?* The message was short but carried a pull he couldn't resist.

He quickly typed back, *Cafeteria. Come join us?*

Anishka stood outside the canteen, clutching her phone as she stared at Ankit's reply. Her stomach twisted—not in the nervous excitement she had once felt when meeting him, but in hesitation. Things between them had grown complicated, and the distance he had created over the past weeks still lingered like a quiet ache. She had thought coming here might clear the air, but now, she wasn't so sure.

Her fingers hovered over her phone. *Maybe I shouldn't have come. What if he brings up the weekend again?* The thought made her chest tighten. She cared about Ankit—he had been her anchor during some of the loneliest days on campus—but his constant need for validation was starting to weigh on her. *Why couldn't he just let things flow?*

With a deep breath, she walked toward the entrance. Her usual confidence felt muted, replaced by a faint anxiety she couldn't quite shake. When she spotted him sitting by the window, his laughter mingling with that of his friends, she hesitated. How could he look so at ease when her own thoughts were a tangled mess?

When Anishka entered, Ankit's eyes immediately found her. She moved with her usual calm grace, but there was something about her today—an undercurrent of uncertainty that wasn't like her. As she approached their table, he sat up a little straighter, his heart quickening in anticipation.

"Hey," she greeted, sliding into the seat beside him. Her voice was light, but her eyes held a depth that hinted at the emotions swirling beneath.

"You're not in class?" she asked, her tone teasing but curious.

"Even I need a break sometimes," Ankit said with a small smile. "The library will forgive me for missing a day."

Ravi leaned forward, grinning. "Witness this moment, Anishka. The mighty Ankit, champion of the library, has finally bunked a class."

They laughed, the lightheartedness lifting the weight Ankit had been carrying. For a moment, it felt like things were normal—like the past few weeks hadn't been filled with avoidance and unanswered questions.

As the conversation flowed, Ankit found himself stealing glances at Anishka. She seemed engaged, laughing at Shubham's jokes and teasing Ravi, but there was a slight tension in her smile—a tightness that only he seemed to notice. He wanted to ask her about it, but every time he tried to find the words, the moment slipped away.

"Hey," he said quietly as the others got lost in their own chatter. "What are you doing this weekend? Maybe we could catch a movie or... just hang out?"

Anishka hesitated, her gaze flickering to the table for a brief second before meeting his. "We'll see, Ankit," she said, her tone nonchalant. "You know how unpredictable my schedule can get."

The casual dismissal stung more than Ankit cared to admit. He nodded, masking his disappointment with a forced smile. "Yeah, of course. Just let me know."

Anishka glanced at her phone, her fingers grazing the screen as she checked a notification. "Sorry, just something from my project group," she murmured, though her attention seemed elsewhere. Ankit tried to ignore the familiar tightening in his chest—the weight of being second place to whatever was on her mind.

As they left the cafeteria and walked across the courtyard, the atmosphere shifted. Ravi and Shubham were engrossed in a heated debate about the upcoming campus festival, their laughter echoing through the open space. Anishka walked beside Ankit, close enough for their shoulders to almost touch, but the gap between them felt vast.

"Ankit, you should perform," she said suddenly, breaking the silence. "I bet you could write something—a poem, maybe. I always thought you had a creative side."

He chuckled, shaking his head. "I think I'll stick to the audience this time. What about you? You could do something with architecture—show off your sketches."

"Oh no," she said, laughing softly. "I'd rather be the one cheering from the sidelines."

Her laugh was light, but her words carried a weight Ankit couldn't ignore. She was retreating again, slipping back into the ambiguity that left him questioning where they stood. He wanted to reach out, to bridge the gap between them, but every time he tried, it felt like she built another wall.

As they reached the library steps, the group paused to discuss plans for the evening. Ankit stayed quiet, his thoughts consumed by the growing distance between him and Anishka. When she finally excused herself, saying she needed to get back to her project, he watched her walk away, her figure disappearing into the crowd.

Walking away, Anishka glanced back once, catching a glimpse of Ankit watching her. A pang of guilt tugged at her chest. *He's going to overthink this again. Why can't he just relax?*

"Sometimes, contentment is a fleeting moment—a fragile peace that fades the moment we question it."

Chapter 12

The Return of Doubt

After lunch, the campus buzzed with life again. The familiar sounds of students chatting, laughing, and shuffling back to their classes filled the air. Ankit walked along the shaded campus paths, taking a deep breath to steady his thoughts. The pressure of final-year decisions weighed heavily on his mind, but for now, he focused on his destination: the placement cell.

As he approached Mrs. Rao's office, his thoughts briefly wandered to how carefree life had been in the earlier years of college. Back then, every decision felt less urgent, less critical. Now, every step felt like it carried the weight of his family's expectations and his future.

Ankit knocked lightly on the office door, the muffled sound of shuffling papers greeting him. Mrs. Rao, surrounded by stacks of folders and notes, looked up with a smile that managed to be both kind and scrutinizing.

"Come in, Ankit. I've been expecting you."

He stepped inside, adjusting the strap of his bag as he sat down. The air in the room felt charged—not with tension, but with the importance of what they were about to discuss. This was about his future, and he couldn't afford to be anything less than prepared.

"How's everything going?" Mrs. Rao asked, her keen eyes fixed on him.

Ankit straightened in his seat, trying to project the confidence he wasn't entirely sure he felt. "Good, ma'am. I've been balancing my studies and preparing for placements. I've also taken on a freelance project—building a portfolio website for a client."

Mrs. Rao nodded approvingly, but her gaze didn't soften. "That's excellent, Ankit. Side projects add depth to your resume. But remember, companies look for more than technical skills. They want to see communication, confidence, and resilience. Can you prove you're ready to deliver on day one?"

Her words struck a chord. Ankit nodded slowly, taking a mental note. "I'll work on that, ma'am. I'll make sure I'm ready."

Mrs. Rao leaned forward slightly, lowering her voice as if to emphasize her next point. "Keep your focus, but don't burn yourself out. Resilience is as much about balance as it is about perseverance. Placements are intense, but don't let the pressure make you lose sight of who you are."

Ankit thanked her and left the office, her advice echoing in his mind. He had known the road ahead would be tough, but her words made it feel both daunting and achievable. As he stepped outside, the warm glow of the afternoon sun met him, but his mind was already shifting to other matters.

His phone buzzed in his pocket, and his heart leapt at the thought of Anishka. Pulling it out, he groaned at the sight of a spam message about a recharge offer. He laughed at the absurdity of his anticipation but couldn't shake the disappointment. Why hadn't she replied yet?

Walking back to his hostel, Ankit's mind raced. She had seemed excited this morning, so why the silence now? Was she second-guessing their weekend plan? His thoughts spiraled as he recalled moments when Anishka had seemed distant, her laughter feeling slightly out of reach, her words laced with an ambiguity that left him unsettled.

Before his doubts could dig deeper, his phone buzzed again. This time, it was her.

"Hey, sorry for the delay. I've thought about it. Let's do the weekend plan. Off-campus sounds good."

Ankit felt his shoulders relax as a grin spread across his face. He stopped mid-step, rereading the message as a wave of relief washed over him. After days of waiting, the anticipation finally gave way to excitement. Quickly, he typed back: "That sounds perfect! How about a movie and dinner?"

"Yeah, sounds good," Anishka replied.

His grin widened, but before he hit send on his next message, he paused, deliberating. Finally, he added, "By the way, could you wear that yellow kurti with the big earrings? You looked stunning in it last time."

A moment passed before her reply arrived—a laughing emoji followed by, "You really notice everything, don't you?"

"Only the important things," he typed back with a playful smirk.

"Alright, I'll wear it," she sent back.

For the first time in weeks, Ankit felt light. This was going to be the perfect weekend, a chance to reconnect and maybe find the clarity he had been searching for. Lying back on his bed later, he stared at the ceiling, replaying their conversation in his mind. But even as excitement bubbled within him, a small voice whispered doubts he couldn't entirely silence.

What if this weekend didn't change anything? What if we're still stuck in this undefined space?

Anishka sat on her bed, her phone still in her hand. She stared at Ankit's last message, her lips curling into a faint smile, but her thoughts weren't as light as her expression.

She liked Ankit. She really did. But lately, his need for constant reassurance was beginning to wear on her. It wasn't something he said outright, but she could feel it in the way he looked at her, in the way he waited for her replies with an eagerness she didn't always know how to reciprocate.

He's going to read so much into this weekend, she thought, placing her phone down beside her. *And I don't even know if I can give him what he wants.*

Her mind flickered to the other plans she was juggling—her projects, her friends, her future. There was too much to think about, too much to handle, and Ankit's emotional reliance was starting to feel like one more thing she couldn't carry.

She sighed, shaking her head. *He'll be thrilled,* she thought, trying to push the guilt aside. *But I can't keep pretending everything's fine.*

Ankit's phone buzzed again as Ravi's text appeared: "Bro, what's the weekend plan? Please tell me you're not studying again."

He smirked and replied, "Nope, no studying. Got plans with Anishka."

"Finally, man! About time you two broke out of the campus bubble," Ravi replied.

Ankit chuckled but felt a pang of uncertainty. As he stared at the screen, excitement battled with a lingering unease. He wanted this weekend to be perfect, but hope, he realized, had a way of making the fall even harder if things didn't work out.

"Sometimes, you find clarity not in the moments you expect, but in the ones where you let go of the need for answers and simply allow life to unfold."

Chapter 13

The Widening Rift

The golden hue of the late afternoon sun trickled through the half-open window, casting soft shadows across the hostel room. Outside, the distant sounds of campus life—students laughing, a cricket ball hitting a bat, the occasional honk of a motorbike—drifted in. But inside Ankit's room, the silence was heavy, like the air before a storm.

Shubham and Ravi, both fresh out of class, strolled toward his door with their usual camaraderie.

Ravi knocked loudly, grinning. "Oi, Romeo! How was the big day with Juliet? Did you sweep her off her feet or what?"

There was no response. The door was ajar, and they caught a glimpse of Ankit sitting on the edge of his bed, his shoulders slumped and his gaze fixed on the floor. His posture, the defeated look on his face—it wasn't what they expected. Ankit, usually the first to crack a joke or lighten the mood, seemed weighed down by something unspoken.

Ravi exchanged a quick glance with Shubham before pushing the door open further. "Bro, what's up with the dead silence?" Shubham asked, stepping inside. "You look like you lost the World Cup."

Ankit stayed quiet for a long moment, his jaw tight. Then, finally, he muttered, “It didn’t go how I thought.”

Ravi plopped down beside him, nudging his shoulder. “What do you mean? You were all pumped up about this weekend. You had that spark, man.”

“I thought it would be... better,” Ankit admitted, his voice flat, almost as if saying the words aloud made them more real.

Shubham pulled up a chair and sat across from him, his tone now serious. “What happened, Ankit? We expected you to come back grinning like an idiot, not... like this.”

Ankit sighed, running a hand through his hair. “We only had two hours.”

“Two hours?” Shubham frowned. “But didn’t you plan the whole day?”

Ankit nodded. “That’s what I thought. But when we met, she told me she had to meet her ‘school best friend’ later. She could only spare a couple of hours.”

Ravi’s playful expression faded. “Her school best friend? Did she say who?”

“She didn’t give a name. Just said it like it was no big deal.” Ankit’s voice grew tight with frustration as he continued. “It’s not about the time. It’s... the way she was with me.”

“What do you mean?” Shubham pressed gently.

Ankit let out a bitter laugh, shaking his head. "She was distracted the whole time. Her phone kept buzzing, and every time she looked at it, it felt like I was... disappearing. She wasn't really there with me."

Shubham leaned forward, his brow furrowing. "And you didn't say anything?"

"What was I supposed to say?" Ankit asked, his voice laced with defeat. "I didn't want to sound needy. I tried to make the most of it. I joked, kept the mood light, but it didn't feel right."

Ravi leaned back, his expression unusually serious. "Did she even realize how you felt?"

"No," Ankit replied, his voice barely above a whisper. "She didn't. She didn't even notice."

The day had started full of promise. Ankit had spent hours planning—beginning with a serene temple visit, followed by lunch at one of the city's best restaurants, and finally, some indoor games at the mall. He'd imagined them laughing, reconnecting, and for a moment, when he saw her, everything felt perfect.

Anishka had looked stunning in the yellow kurti he had asked her to wear, her big earrings catching the sunlight as she smiled. But soon after they met, she mentioned her other plans with a casualness that stung more than she probably realized.

"It's only a couple of hours," she had said, her tone breezy. "We'll still have plenty of time together."

Ankit had tried to brush off the discomfort. He didn't want to seem clingy. But as the hours passed, her distant smiles and the way her fingers hovered near her phone told a different story. At lunch, her laughter felt forced, her attention fragmented. Every message she received seemed to pull her further away, and Ankit was left trying to fill the growing gap with small talk and strained jokes.

Back in the room, the silence between the friends deepened. Shubham finally broke it, his tone firm. "You need to talk to her, Ankit. This isn't healthy."

"What if talking makes things worse?" Ankit asked, his voice heavy with doubt. "What if she pulls away even more?"

"You can't keep living in 'what if,'" Ravi chimed in. "Either you clear the air, or this is going to eat you alive."

Ankit stared at the floor, the weight of their words settling over him. "She said we'd plan something next weekend," he said softly. "But I don't know. I don't know if anything will change."

Shubham stood, placing a hand on Ankit's shoulder. "You've got to try, bro. Before it's too late."

Ravi nodded. "And if she doesn't see what you bring to her life... well, that's on her. Not you."

Ankit forced a weak smile, appreciating their support, but the heaviness in his chest remained. As the sun set, casting long shadows across the room, he realized that the bond he and Anishka once shared wasn't just strained—it was slipping away.

"Sometimes, the hardest part of losing someone isn't the goodbye—it's the slow drift away, the silences where there used to be words".

"The worst kind of loneliness is standing right next to someone and feeling like they're a thousand miles away."

Chapter 14

Shattered Bonds

The faint morning light filtered through the cracks in the hostel curtains as Ankit sat at his desk, staring at his phone. He reread Anishka's last message from days ago, her words feeling more distant with each passing moment. The warmth they had once shared seemed fragile now, slipping through his fingers like sand.

From the previous week's conversation, he had tried to hold onto hope. She had promised to make things better after their short and fragmented weekend together. But promises, Ankit was starting to realize, meant little without follow-through.

His thoughts circled back to the closing conversation with Shubham and Ravi from a few nights ago—their push for him to confront the growing distance between him and Anishka. Yet, the words still stuck in his throat. He feared that speaking them aloud might solidify what he had been trying to ignore.

Ankit forced himself into the rhythm of the day. By mid-morning, he was in the cafeteria, nursing a steaming cup of chai. Around him, the familiar hum of college life carried on, students laughing, trading notes, and planning their weekends. Normally, this energy would have lifted his spirits, but today, it only highlighted the void.

His phone buzzed, and his heart jumped—Anishka's name flashed on the screen. He unlocked his phone with shaky hands, reading her message.

"Hey, sorry for the silence. Been swamped with projects and family stuff. Let's meet soon, okay?"

A part of him relaxed at her response, but another part—one that had been growing louder lately—reminded him of the pattern. This wasn't the first time she had brushed him off with vague reasons. He sighed, typing back quickly.

"It's okay. I get it. Let me know when you're free."

He hesitated before hitting send, debating whether to ask her directly about her distance. But the fear of pushing her further away stopped him. For now, he would take whatever connection he could get, even if it felt like scraps of what they once had.

By the afternoon, Ankit found himself sitting with Shubham and Ravi in their usual corner of the library. The two were bantering about Garba Night, the event everyone was buzzing about.

"Falguni Pathak, man!" Ravi exclaimed. "It's going to be epic! And you, Mr. Lover Boy, have your date all set, right?"

Ankit smiled weakly, not wanting to dampen their excitement. "Yeah, Anishka and I talked about it a while back."

Shubham looked up from his notes, raising an eyebrow. "You sure about that? She's been kinda... distant, hasn't she?"

Ankit bristled, not because Shubham was wrong, but because the truth was becoming harder to ignore. "She's just busy," he replied, though the words sounded hollow even to himself. "We'll figure it out."

Around them, students discussed Garba Night with infectious excitement. Girls whispered about coordinating outfits—lehenga cholis in vibrant colors, bright bangles that would jingle with every twirl—while the boys argued over who would outshine whom on the dance floor. The campus seemed to come alive during these cultural events, offering a break from the grind of assignments and exams.

For Ankit, these nights were more than just events.

"In a world of classes, deadlines, and uncertain futures, nights like Garba Night felt like lifelines—moments to hold onto something brighter."

For a fleeting moment, he allowed himself to believe that Garba Night could be the reset he and Anishka needed.

That evening, as Ankit sat in his room scrolling aimlessly through Instagram, his phone buzzed with an incoming call. It was Anishka.

"Hey," he answered quickly, his voice betraying a mix of relief and nervousness.

"Hi," she replied, her tone soft but distant. "Sorry I've been MIA. Things have been crazy."

"It's okay," Ankit said, trying to keep his tone light. "I just missed talking to you."

There was a pause on the other end, long enough for Ankit to wonder if she had heard him. Then, she spoke, her voice slightly warmer. "I missed you too. I've just had a lot going on."

The knot in his stomach loosened slightly, though the hesitation in her words lingered. "So, Garba Night?" he ventured, his voice filled with cautious optimism. "We're still going together, right?"

Anishka's voice brightened. "Of course! I promised, didn't I? I've even picked out something special for us."

For a moment, everything felt normal again. Ankit latched onto her enthusiasm, letting it wash away his doubts. *But there was something about the way she said it.*

"Her tone brightened as she promised, but there was a hollowness behind her words—like she was giving just enough to keep him holding on."

As the night deepened, Ankit's optimism began to waver. Sitting on his bed, he replayed their conversation in his head. Something about it felt rehearsed, as though she were saying what she thought he wanted to hear.

The way her voice had faltered, the slight delay in her responses—it all gnawed at him.

He stared at his phone, debating whether to text her again. But what would he say? The more he tried to make sense of her actions, the more confused he became. Was he reading too much into things? Or was there something she wasn't telling him?

His mind flickered back to her mention of being "swamped." What did that mean? Family, projects, or something—or someone—else? He hated the paranoia creeping in, but the gaps in their connection left too much room for his imagination to run wild.

Finally, he set his phone down, forcing himself to focus on the promise of Garba Night. It was their chance to reset, to reconnect. Maybe, just maybe, things would feel right again.

"Sometimes, hope is all we have. But hope, without clarity, can become a heavy burden."

PART 5

THE FALL AND THE SILENCE

Chapter 15

The Breaking Point

The next morning, the campus was buzzing. Posters for Garba Night were everywhere—colorful, vibrant, and promising an unforgettable evening. This wasn't just any college event; the whispers that Falguni Pathak herself would perform had transformed it into something larger than life.

The news spread like wildfire, igniting excitement across lecture halls, hostel rooms, and WhatsApp groups. It was the kind of event that students would talk about for years, and for Ankit, it brought back a flicker of hope.

For days, he had carried the weight of silence—Anishka's missed calls, unread messages, and the growing distance that gnawed at him. But now, as Garba Night loomed, he clung to one thing: her promise. *She said we'd go together,* he reminded himself.

Ankit leaned against the cool wall outside his classroom, scrolling through the messages in his class group:

"Falguni Pathak! I'm not missing this for anything."

"Booked my outfit—who's practicing their dandiya moves with me?"

"Bro, do you even know the steps, or will you do bhangra instead?"

The buzz was contagious, and for a brief moment, Ankit let it seep into him. He smiled faintly, recalling the light-hearted conversation he'd once had with Anishka.

"Garba Night sounds amazing! I've never been, but I'm all in," she had said, her voice full of excitement.

"You? Dancing? You'll trip in the first five minutes," he'd teased, unable to stop smiling.

"I'll prove you wrong," she had challenged. "I'll even bring you an outfit—no excuses."

That moment replayed in his mind like a distant memory, and the thought of her smile was enough to soften the ache in his chest. *We'll own Garba Night,* he had promised.

But today was different. Her silence was louder than ever.

Ankit sat with Shubham and Ravi at the hostel snack bar. The air was thick with the smell of chai, samosas, and the excited chatter of students making their Garba plans.

"So, what's the plan for the big night?" Ravi grinned, his voice carrying its usual mischief. "You and Anishka are still the headline act, right?"

Shubham smirked. "The two of you will be inseparable in those matching outfits, man. Bollywood couple vibes."

Ankit forced a laugh, though it didn't quite reach his eyes. "Yeah, we talked about it... she said we'd go together."

Shubham caught the hesitation in his voice. "You sound unsure. What's up?"

Ankit hesitated, his fingers tracing the edge of his cup. "I don't know, guys. She's been... distant. I haven't heard from her in two days. No replies, nothing."

Ravi frowned, setting down his cup. "Two days? That's weird. Did you try calling her?"

Ankit nodded, his voice quieter now. "Yeah. Nothing."

Shubham, ever the optimist, clapped Ankit on the back. "Relax, man. You know Anishka. She's probably caught up with something. You'll see—Garba Night will fix everything."

Will it? Ankit thought. But he nodded anyway, trying to force himself to believe it.

Lying in his bed, the silence was unbearable. Ankit stared at his phone screen, reading their old messages—the laughter, the plans, the promises.

"We'll make this Garba Night one to remember."

The words echoed in his mind, but now they felt hollow.

How did I let myself believe this? he wondered, his chest tightening. *Hadn't she been slipping away for weeks?*

Unable to sleep, Ankit dragged himself to the common room where Ravi and Shubham were sprawled out on the beanbags. The hostel lights flickered dimly, and the hum of ceiling fans blended with murmurs of late-night chatter.

"Ankit, you're still awake?" Ravi asked, throwing a crumpled packet of chips at him playfully. "What's going on, man? Big Garba Night jitters?"

Ankit gave a weak smile and sank into the old chair beside them. "Can't sleep. Just thinking about stuff."

Shubham, always the blunt one, cut to the chase. "Thinking about Anishka or placements? Because dude, you need to get your act together. You missed Rao ma'am's placement session yesterday, and people are starting to notice."

Ravi nodded, his tone more careful. "Yeah, man. Everyone's saying the class topper is distracted these days. Even that Sharma guy—the one who lives for gossip—was telling people you're not even finishing assignments on time."

Ankit looked down at his hands, the weight of their words settling heavily in his chest. "I know, okay? I'll catch up. I've just been... dealing with some stuff."

Shubham groaned, tossing his pen on the floor. "Come on, Ankit! Placements are next month. You don't have time to 'deal with stuff.' You're the guy everyone looks up to in class—don't let some girl derail everything you've worked for."

Ankit's jaw tightened, his eyes fixed on the worn-out carpet beneath his feet. "It's not just about her," he murmured, though even he didn't believe it.

Ravi sighed, his tone softer now. "We get it. College isn't easy, and neither are relationships. But you can't lose yourself like this. If something's wrong, fix it, man. Before it's too late."

Their words stung because they were true. For the past few weeks, Ankit had been slipping—skipping study sessions, falling behind on assignments, and losing focus during lectures. The topper everyone admired was starting to crack under the weight of his own emotions.

As Ravi and Shubham fell into quieter conversation about Garba Night plans, Ankit stared at his phone once again, scrolling through his texts with Anishka. Her last message replayed in his mind: *"I promised, didn't I?"*

He wanted to believe her.

But somewhere deep down, he wondered if he was clinging to a memory of her—one that no longer matched the person she was now.

The amphitheater was alive with color and sound. Students twirled in vibrant chaniya cholis and kurtas, their laughter and cheers rising above the pounding beats of the dhol. Falguni Pathak's voice soared through the cool evening air, igniting the crowd with every note.

Ankit stood at the entrance, dressed in the outfit Anishka had helped him pick out. His heart raced—not with excitement but with anticipation tainted by nerves. He glanced at his phone. Still no messages.

He dialed her number.

No answer.

He tried again, his palms dampening as his chest grew tight. The music, the laughter, the joy of the crowd—it all seemed to blur around him.

Where is she?

Minutes turned to an hour. Ankit stood frozen in the chaos, his eyes scanning the crowd for her face. Every passing moment felt heavier, like stones piling onto his heart.

He dialed her roommate's number, desperation now gnawing at him. No answer there, either.

The music pounded in his ears, but all Ankit could hear was the silence of her absence. The crowd moved like waves, their energy rising and falling with the rhythm. But for Ankit, every beat of the dhol felt like a hammer on his chest—louder than the unanswered calls.

"Garba Night will fix everything," Shubham had said.

But as he stood there, alone in the middle of it all, those words felt like a cruel joke.

"Sometimes, the moments we look forward to the most are the ones that never happen. And in their absence, we realize that hope, when stretched too thin, can tear us apart.

Chapter 16

The Weight of Silence

The night after Garba Night was unbearable for Ankit. He lay motionless on his bed, staring at the cracked ceiling of his hostel room. The muffled sounds of laughter and chatter from the hallway seeped through the door, but they felt distant, like echoes from a world he no longer belonged to. His heart felt heavy, an anchor pulling him deeper into despair.

Every few minutes, his eyes darted to his phone on the bedside table. He had checked it a hundred times already, hoping for a missed call or a message from Anishka, but the screen stayed stubbornly blank. He fought the urge to call her again, afraid of more silence. The memories of Garba Night haunted him—the outfit she had picked out for him, the promises they had made, and the moment Ravi told him she was there... but with someone else.

Ankit buried his face in his hands, a deep, guttural sob breaking through the silence. It wasn't just heartbreak—it was humiliation, confusion, and a deep sense of betrayal. He felt like a fool for believing in her words, her promises. The girl who had been the center of his world had shattered it in the cruelest way.

The next morning, Ankit woke to a hollow ache in his chest. The bright sunlight streaming through the window felt like a cruel joke. The world had moved on, but he was stuck in a loop of pain and unanswered questions. His phone was still devoid of any messages or calls from Anishka.

As he stepped out of his room, the hostel corridors buzzed with energy. Groups of students gathered, chatting about last night's Garba Night. The excitement and gossip felt like needles pricking Ankit's skin.

"Did you see Anishka and Akash last night?" someone whispered as he passed by. "They looked like such a perfect couple."

"Poor Ankit," another voice added, not bothering to lower their tone. "Everyone thought he'd be with her, but Akash swooped in."

Ankit clenched his fists, his nails digging into his palms. The words stung more than he wanted to admit. He walked faster, trying to escape the whispers, but they seemed to follow him wherever he went.

At the canteen, Shubham and Ravi were waiting for him. Their faces were serious, their usual banter replaced with concern.

"Bro, sit down," Shubham said softly, motioning to an empty chair. "We need to talk."

Ankit hesitated but eventually sat down. He couldn't avoid this conversation forever.

"What happened last night?" Shubham asked gently. "Why didn't you come to Garba?"

Ankit sighed, staring at the untouched plate of food in front of him. "She didn't pick up my calls. I tried so many times, but she just... ignored me."

Ravi exchanged a glance with Shubham before speaking. "Ankit, we didn't want to tell you like this, but... we saw her."

Ankit's head snapped up, his eyes wide with disbelief. "What do you mean?"

"She was there," Ravi said carefully. "With Akash. They were together the whole night."

Ankit's stomach dropped. His hands trembled as he tried to process the words. "No... that can't be true. She promised me. She said we'd go together."

"Ankit," Shubham said, placing a comforting hand on his shoulder. "We're sorry, man. But it's true. She was with him. People said Akash even proposed to her two days ago."

The words hit Ankit like a freight train. His mind reeled, replaying every moment of the past few weeks—her vague answers, the missed calls, the growing distance. It all made sense now. She had been pulling away because she had already chosen someone else.

Ankit's thoughts spiraled as he stumbled back to his room. He slammed the door shut, leaning against it as tears streamed down his face. The weight of betrayal was suffocating. He had trusted her, cared for her, believed in her promises—and she had shattered all of it without a second thought.

"Was I not good enough?" he whispered to the empty room. "Did I do something wrong?"

He threw himself onto his bed, burying his face in his pillow. The pain was overwhelming, but beneath it all, a flicker of anger began to rise. How could she do this to him? How could she string him along while entertaining someone else? Memories of her sweet messages and playful teasing now felt like cruel lies.

Later that afternoon, Ankit overheard more whispers outside his room.

"Did you hear? Anishka told people she was never serious about Ankit. She said he got too attached."

"Akash and Anishka make a much better couple. He's got that Google internship lined up. Way out of Ankit's league."

The words were like daggers. Ankit wanted to scream, to tell them they were wrong, but deep down, he knew they weren't. Anishka had been pulling the strings all along, and he had been too blind to see it.

Unable to contain his emotions, Ankit picked up his phone and dialed her number. It rang and rang, but there was no answer. He tried again, his desperation growing with each failed attempt. Finally, after what felt like an eternity, she picked up.

"Ankit, I—" she started, but he cut her off.

"Why, Anishka?" he demanded, his voice shaking with emotion. "Why did you lie to me? Why did you promise me Garba Night when you knew you were going with Akash?"

There was a long pause on the other end. "I didn't mean to hurt you," she said softly. "Things just... happened."

"Things just happened?" Ankit repeated bitterly. "Do you even realize what you've done to me? Do you even care?"

"I do care," she said, but her voice lacked conviction. "But I didn't know how to tell you."

"Tell me what?" Ankit asked, his voice rising. "That I was just a backup plan? That you were never serious about us?"

"Ankit, please," she said, her tone pleading. "I didn't mean for it to end like this."

"But it did," Ankit replied, his voice breaking. "And now I have to live with it."

He ended the call before she could respond, his hands trembling as he set the phone down. The silence that followed was deafening, but for the first time, it felt like closure. Ankit knew he couldn't keep holding on to someone who had already let go of him.

That night, Ankit sat alone under a tree on campus, staring at the dark sky. The stars were hidden behind thick clouds, but he didn't mind. The emptiness he felt was strangely liberating. He had given his all to someone who didn't value it, but now, he was ready to move on.

"Sometimes," he whispered to himself, "the only way to heal is to let go."

"The hardest battles are fought within, and sometimes, walking away is the bravest thing you can do."

PART 6

THE ART OF LETTING GO

Chapter 17

Picking Up the Pieces

The morning light filtered through Ankit's curtains, but it did little to warm him. His room, once a haven of peace and order, now felt suffocating. Books, clothes, and half-empty coffee cups cluttered the floor. His bed was an unmade mess of crumpled sheets, reflecting the chaos inside his mind. It had been two weeks since Anishka had blocked him. Two weeks since he had heard her voice, seen her messages, or even caught a glimpse of her in passing. And in those two weeks, Ankit had fallen apart.

The regularity and routine he once prided himself on—his disciplined morning study sessions, his carefully organized notes for upcoming placements—had all slipped away. Instead, the only thing that consumed him now was her. Anishka. She occupied every corner of his mind, and no matter how hard he tried, he couldn't shake the ache of her absence.

Ankit recapped the memory of their last real conversation, the weekend when everyone had left for a short break and the campus had fallen silent. They had sat in the empty garden for hours, watching the evening sky fade into night, talking about everything and nothing. That weekend had felt special, like a private moment just for the two of them.

"You know," she had said, her voice soft but full of warmth, "I've always liked this place. It's peaceful when no one's around."

Ankit had smiled. "Yeah, it feels like we have the whole world to ourselves."

They had laughed then, about silly things—about how most students were already on their way home for the holidays, how they had nowhere to be, and how that emptiness made the campus feel like their personal retreat. For three or four days, it was just them, spending time together, talking late into the night. Ankit remembered her laughing as they wandered through the dimly lit pathways of the garden.

It was the first time he had really felt connected to someone like that. He could tell she had felt it too—or so he had believed. *What changed?* Ankit thought for the hundredth time. *Did I say something wrong? Did I misread her feelings?* The questions circled in his mind, each one more tormenting than the last.

He had replayed every conversation they'd had, searching for clues. *Was it that time I didn't text her back immediately? Maybe she thought I didn't care. Or was it the night we argued about Garba Night? Did I come off as too pushy?* The lack of answers gnawed at him, driving him deeper into his despair.

Ankit hadn't left his room in days. He hadn't attended a single class, ignored every message from Shubham and Ravi, and had even stopped checking his emails. His phone buzzed a few times, notifications lighting up the screen, but he ignored them. All that mattered was figuring out what had gone wrong with Anishka.

He had tried calling her, over and over again. From different numbers, from Shubham's phone, Ravi's phone, even payphones he found near campus. Each time, the result was the same: blocked. Anishka wasn't just ignoring him—she had shut him out completely. That realization had broken him, and he had sunk deeper into isolation.

The mental strain was unbearable. His mind spun with thoughts, memories, and regrets. His friends' calls went unanswered, the pile of assignments on his desk grew larger, and his Gmail inbox was overflowing with unread messages. He had disconnected from everyone—his friends, his parents, even himself. The world outside kept moving, but Ankit was stuck, lost in a spiral of his own making.

His room had become a prison. Days passed in a blur. The only moments that stood out were the ones when he recapped his memories of Anishka—the good ones, the bad ones, and all the ones in between. Every time his mind wandered, it brought him back to her. He could still hear her laugh, still see her smile, still feel the weight of the conversations they used to have. But now, all of it felt tainted, like a cruel trick his mind was playing on him.

The campus was buzzing with excitement over the upcoming placement drives. Companies were starting to visit for pre-placement talks, and the air was thick with anticipation. But Ankit, once the most focused and driven student in his class, was barely aware of it. His grades had slipped, his professors had noticed his absences, and the opportunities that were once within his grasp were starting to slip away.

One evening, Shubham and Ravi managed to get into his room. They had been worried about him for days, but every time they tried to reach him, they were met with silence. Now, standing in the mess of Ankit's room, they could see just how far their friend had fallen.

"Bro, what's going on?" Shubham asked, his voice a mix of concern and frustration. "You've missed so many classes. You didn't even fill out the application for the placement drive. The test is tomorrow."

Ankit barely reacted. His eyes remained fixed on the wall, his thoughts still on Anishka.

"Ankit, did you hear me?" Ravi asked, trying to get through to him. "The company that's coming tomorrow is huge. It's a big opportunity. You need to get it together."

But Ankit just shook his head. "I don't care."

Shubham exchanged a worried glance with Ravi. "You don't care? About placements? About your future? What the hell happened to you?"

Ankit finally looked at them, his face pale, his eyes hollow. "She blocked me," he said quietly. "She blocked me on everything."

There was a long silence. Shubham sighed, rubbing the back of his neck. "Ankit, I get it. But you can't let this destroy you. Placements are happening whether you're ready or not. You can't throw your future away because of her."

The next day, Shubham and Ravi left for the placement test without Ankit. They had tried one last time to convince him to join them, but he had refused. As the hours passed, Ankit sat alone in his room, staring at the unopened university email on his phone. He knew it was too late. The test had already started, and there was nothing he could do now.

By the time the results were posted, Ankit had completely shut down. Shubham and Ravi returned to the hostel, their faces tense with excitement and nervous energy.

"Ravi made it to the final round," Shubham announced, his voice full of pride.

Ankit nodded, barely registering the words.

"You could have been there too, man," Ravi said, his tone softer. "You had a real shot."

But Ankit didn't respond. The weight of his choices—or lack of them—pressed down on him, and for the first time in weeks, he began to realize just how much he had lost.

"Sometimes, the pieces we lose aren't just parts of a broken heart—they're pieces of ourselves we may never get back."

Chapter 18

Acceptance and Release

The sun hung low in the sky, the soft golden hue casting long shadows across Ankit's dorm room. By now, the warmth of a new day had faded into a numbing routine of isolation. His once-pristine room, a testament to his meticulous nature, now resembled a battlefield—clothes strewn across the floor, untouched books gathering dust, and a pile of unopened university emails silently accusing him of neglect.

The excitement of Ravi's placement breakthrough was palpable throughout the hostel, yet it barely registered with Ankit.

"Ankit, I made it! I got the offer—13 LPA from Coco Software!" Ravi exclaimed, bursting into the room, his voice filled with the kind of joy that once would have made Ankit leap from his seat to celebrate.

Instead, Ankit barely looked up. "Congrats, man," he muttered, his tone devoid of any energy.

Ravi's excitement faltered. This wasn't the Ankit he knew. His once-driven, focused friend was now a shadow of himself.

"Thanks... but seriously, what's going on with you?" Ravi asked cautiously, concern etching his features.

Ankit stared at the floor, the memories of the past few weeks flooding his mind. It wasn't just about Anishka anymore—it was everything. The overwhelming pressure of placements, the expectations of his parents, and the crushing weight of his emotional struggles had coalesced into a suffocating storm.

"I'm fine. Just... a lot on my mind," Ankit replied.

"Fine?" Ravi shot back, his concern morphing into frustration. "You've missed weeks of class. Shubham and I have been worried sick about you!"

Ankit gave a weak smile, trying to placate Ravi, but deep down, he knew his friend was right. The world was moving forward, and he was stuck, unable—or unwilling—to take the first step.

Meanwhile, Shubham's frustration had been building for weeks. He had watched Ankit slip further into despair, his once-promising future unraveling in front of him. That evening, he stormed into Ankit's room without knocking, his anger finally boiling over.

"Ankit, what the hell are you doing?" Shubham's voice cut through the heavy silence like a whip.

Ankit barely glanced up, his expression blank. "I'm figuring things out," he replied weakly.

"Figuring things out? You're throwing your entire life away because of one girl!" Shubham's voice was rising. "Do you even know why Anishka blocked you?"

Ankit froze. The question hit him like a slap, his heart pounding in his chest. "What do you mean?"

Shubham took a deep breath, trying to contain his frustration. "Do you know Priya? Anishka's roommate?"

Ankit nodded slowly, unsure of where this was going.

"Well, Priya told me something. Anishka felt you were getting too emotionally attached. She wasn't ready for that kind of commitment. You pushed her to go to Garba Night even though she didn't want to, and she agreed because she felt guilty. She didn't want to hurt you."

Ankit's chest tightened. The words stung, but he forced himself to listen.

"There's more," Shubham continued. "A few months ago, she started talking to Akash—the guy doing a Google internship. They've been meeting up on campus and spending hours talking, especially at night. Remember when she used to cut your calls, saying she was busy talking to school friends? She wasn't. She was talking to Akash."

Ankit's heart sank. He felt a mix of anger, betrayal, and shame, but Shubham wasn't finished.

"Priya said Anishka is ambitious. She wants to work at Google or companies like that. Akash is her way to get closer to that dream. She didn't come to Garba Night because Akash approached her that morning, and she chose to spend the day with him."

Ankit stared at Shubham, his mind reeling. He felt like the ground had been ripped out from under him. Everything he had believed about their relationship—every laugh, every shared moment—felt like a cruel joke.

"But why block me?" Ankit whispered, his voice trembling.

"Because she didn't know how to deal with your feelings," Shubham said bluntly. "She thought cutting you off completely would make it easier for both of you."

Ankit buried his face in his hands, his emotions boiling over. Betrayal. Anger. Confusion. It was too much to process.

Shubham's voice softened as he saw the pain in Ankit's eyes. "Look, man, I know this hurts. But you can't let one person define your entire life. She's made her choices, and now you need to make yours. Placements are happening. Your parents are worried. Ravi and I are worried. You're letting everything fall apart because you're stuck in the past."

Ankit stood up, his emotions erupting like a volcano. "You think I can just forget her? You think this is easy?"

"No, I don't," Shubham shot back. "But I also don't think you get to sit here and wallow while your future slips away. You're better than this, Ankit. You've always been better than this."

Ankit's anger dissolved into sadness, tears streaming down his face. "I don't know how to let go, Shubham. I don't know how to move on."

Shubham placed a hand on Ankit's shoulder, his voice firm but kind. "You don't have to do it alone. We're here for you. But you have to take the first step."

Ankit nodded slowly, the weight of Shubham's words settling over him. The road ahead was uncertain, but for the first time, he felt like he wasn't entirely alone.

As the room fell into silence, Ankit looked out the window, the stars twinkling against the inky black sky. The memories of Anishka still lingered, but Shubham's words had planted a seed—a faint glimmer of hope that maybe, just maybe, he could find a way to move forward.

"Sometimes, the hardest battles aren't fought on the outside. They're fought within, in the quiet moments of despair, when we decide whether to give up or push forward."

Chapter 19

Breaking Free

The last few days had been some of the toughest in Ankit's life. The heated argument with Shubham had forced him to confront the truth he had been avoiding for weeks—he was stuck, emotionally trapped in a loop of pain and memories. While the fight had hurt, it also felt like a release, cracking open the walls he had built around himself. For the first time in weeks, he allowed himself to truly feel—not just the pain, but also the faint glimmer of something he hadn't felt in a long time: hope.

That morning felt different. The sunlight streaming through the curtains didn't carry the weight it usually did. Ankit opened his eyes and noticed his cluttered room—the books scattered across the desk, the crumpled notes, and the untouched pile of laundry. The sight, which had once overwhelmed him, now seemed like an invitation to start over.

Rising from bed, he noticed a neatly wrapped package Shubham and Ravi had left the night before. The Bhagavad Gita lay on his desk, along with a handwritten note. Ankit unfolded the paper, his heart quickening as he read:

Hey Ankit,

We know things have been tough, and we're sorry for the fight. But bro, it's time to let go. It's time to break free. We believe in you—always.

Shubham & Ravi

The words hit him like a wave. He hadn't realized just how much his friends had been observing him, how much they cared. His throat tightened as he carefully opened the package, revealing the book inside. It wasn't just any gift—it was a reminder of something he had started but never finished, something he had put aside when life became overwhelming.

Ankit sat down with the book in his hands, feeling its weight. It reminded him of conversations with his father, who had always spoken about the power of the Gita, how its teachings could guide one through the darkest of times. Ankit hadn't taken those words seriously before, but now, holding the book in this moment, it felt like a lifeline.

He opened it to the first chapter, his fingers grazing over the pages. As he read through the verses, words of duty, purpose, and detachment stood out. The teachings of Lord Krishna echoed in his mind, and for the first time in weeks, he felt grounded. One verse, in particular, resonated deeply with him:

"You have the right to perform your duty, but you are not entitled to the fruits of your actions. Let go of the attachment to results."

This was what he needed to hear. He had been so consumed by what he had lost, so attached to the outcome of his relationship with Anishka, that he had forgotten the importance of focusing on his own actions—on what he could control. He pinned the note and the quote to his wall as reminders.

The gift and note stirred something inside him. It wasn't an immediate transformation, but it gave him the courage to take the first small step. That afternoon, Ankit decided to clean his room. As he picked up the books and papers scattered across the floor, he couldn't help but notice the layers of dust that had settled on everything. It mirrored his life—abandoned and neglected.

By the time he finished, his desk was clear, his bed was made, and the room felt... lighter. He sat down and opened his laptop for the first time in weeks. His inbox was flooded with emails—placement updates, missed deadlines, and messages from professors. The sheer volume was overwhelming, but instead of closing it, he decided to tackle one email at a time.

The first email was from his placement coordinator, reminding him about an upcoming company visit. His heart sank as he realized how much time he had wasted. But instead of dwelling on regret, he made a decision: *I'll attend the next one.* It wasn't about impressing anyone or proving himself—it was about taking responsibility for his future.

The next day, Ankit went to the library to prepare for placements. Walking through the quiet halls brought back memories—each corner of the library held a piece of his past with Anishka. As he turned a corner, he froze.

There she was.

Anishka was sitting at a table with Akash, the final-year topper and Google intern. Their heads were close, and they were laughing softly, oblivious to the world around them. Ankit's heart clenched, the sight triggering a surge of emotions—pain, jealousy, and anger all at once. He felt like turning around, retreating before they noticed him.

But something stopped him. He stood there for a moment, letting the emotions rise. The old Ankit would have spiraled, but now, he took a deep breath and reminded himself of the verses from the Gita. *Detachment does not mean you should own nothing, but that nothing should own you.*

She's moved on, and so can I, he thought. The realization didn't erase the pain, but it softened the edges, making it bearable. Without another glance, he walked away, his steps steady and purposeful. For the first time, he felt a sense of closure—not from her, but from himself.

That evening, Ankit sat with Shubham and Ravi in their dorm. For weeks, he had avoided their conversations, but now, he felt ready to reconnect.

"Dude, you're cleaning your room now?" Shubham teased, glancing at the newly organized desk. "Who are you, and what have you done with Ankit?"

Ankit chuckled, the sound surprising even himself. "I guess I just got tired of living in a mess."

Shubham nodded, his tone softening. "We're glad to see you back, man. It's been rough watching you go through this."

"I know," Ankit admitted. "And I'm sorry for shutting you guys out. I didn't know how to handle everything."

Ravi clapped him on the shoulder. "You don't have to do it alone. That's what we're here for."

The conversation shifted to placements, and for the first time, Ankit felt excited about the future. He made a plan to attend the next pre-placement talk and even signed up for a coding competition. It wasn't about winning—it was about rediscovering the parts of himself he had lost.

Before going to bed, Ankit opened his notebook and wrote down a new goal: *Prepare for placements with focus and determination.* Below it, he added the quote from the Gita: *"Let go of the attachment to results."*

He stuck the paper on the wall above his desk, a daily reminder of his journey forward.

The next morning, as Ankit walked across the campus, he felt a quiet sense of peace. The world hadn't changed, but he had. The weight of the past was still there, but it no longer defined him. He was no longer waiting for someone else to bring him closure—he had found it within himself.

Ankit knew the road ahead wouldn't be easy. There would be moments of doubt, times when the pain resurfaced. But now, he felt equipped to face them. He had his friends, his family, and most importantly, his own strength.

As the sun set that evening, painting the sky in hues of orange and pink, Ankit stood by the window of his dorm room. For the first time in months, he felt free.

"Sometimes, breaking free isn't about forgetting the past—it's about choosing to move forward despite it."

PART 7

HEALING AND RISING ABOVE

Chapter 20

Healing Through Reflection

The placement hall buzzed with tension, the low hum of whispered conversations blending with the soft clatter of keyboards. The final-year students were deep into their coding tests, each keystroke carrying the weight of their futures. Ankit sat among them, hunched over his laptop, his face drawn with concentration—or at least an attempt at it. The problem on his screen stared back at him, unsolvable in his eyes, despite the hours he had poured into preparation.

The invigilator's voice rang out. "Five minutes left!"

Ankit's hands hovered over the keyboard, the pressure mounting. He had spent weeks brushing up on algorithms and data structures, but now, his mind felt like a blank canvas. Anxiety gnawed at him. With a resigned sigh, he typed a partial solution, knowing it wasn't enough. When the timer hit zero, he closed his laptop, his stomach churning with disappointment.

The murmurs around him grew louder as students exited the hall. Some were already dissecting the test, comparing answers, while others wore stoic expressions, masking their anxiety. Ankit walked out silently, his confidence further eroded. This was his fifth rejection in two weeks, and the sting of failure was beginning to feel unbearable.

Back in his dorm room, the familiar chaos greeted him. Books and notes lay scattered on his desk, a testament to his frantic study sessions. His bed, unmade for days, mirrored the disarray in his mind. Shubham sat on his side of the room, poring over notes for his upcoming interview with a prestigious multinational firm. Ravi, on the other hand, was busy celebrating his recent offer from Coco Software, his laughter echoing down the corridor as friends congratulated him.

Ankit sank into his chair, his eyes drifting to the pinboard above his desk. It was filled with motivational quotes and plans he had written at the start of placement season. *"Stay focused,"* one note read. Another said, *"Every rejection is a step closer to success."* But now, those words felt hollow.

His phone buzzed with yet another notification from a college WhatsApp group: *"Congratulations to all those who cleared today's technical round!"* Ankit didn't bother opening it.

The pressure wasn't just from within—it was everywhere. His family, though supportive, would often ask, *"How's the placement process going, beta?"* His friends, unintentionally, added to the weight with their successes. Every rejection chipped away at his self-esteem, leaving him questioning his worth.

That evening, unable to bear the noise of celebration in the corridor, Ankit retreated to the terrace. The cool breeze brushed against his face, a stark contrast to the storm raging within him. He pulled out his phone, scrolling through old photos in a futile attempt to find solace.

One picture stopped him. It was of him and Anishka, taken during a campus fest. She was laughing, her head tilted back, and he was mid-sentence, caught in a candid moment. Her energy had been magnetic, her presence a light in his life during those days.

"Why did everything fall apart?" he whispered, his voice barely audible.

Memories flooded back—her encouraging texts before exams, their late-night conversations about dreams and fears, and the warmth she brought into his life. But those memories, once a source of comfort, now felt like salt on an open wound.

For weeks, he had avoided confronting his pain, but tonight, it was unavoidable. He pulled out the notebook he had once used for brainstorming projects and began writing:

- *Why wasn't I enough?*
- *What did I do wrong?*
- *Why did she leave without a proper goodbye?*

The words poured out like a dam breaking. As he filled the pages, his questions began to shift:

- *What do I deserve in a relationship?*
- *What kind of person do I want to be?*
- *How can I rebuild myself?*

The act of writing was cathartic. It wasn't a solution, but it was a start—a small step toward understanding himself.

Back in his room, Ankit decided it was time to create a space for himself—a corner of solace amidst the chaos. He cleared his desk, placing his well-worn copy of the *Bhagavad Gita* in the center. Around it, he stuck sticky notes with quotes that had resonated with him:

- *"Focus on actions, not results."*
- *"Let go of attachment to outcomes."*
- *"Every challenge is an opportunity to grow."*

The quotes were reminders of the lessons he was trying to internalize. He created a small board for reflection, pinning his thoughts and lessons learned. It wasn't much, but it symbolized his commitment to move forward.

He also revisited his love for coding—not for placements, but for himself. Opening his laptop, Ankit began working on a personal project: a website to document his journey. He titled one section *Reflections*, where he uploaded snippets of his thoughts and the lessons he had learned.

One night, as Ankit worked on his website, Shubham walked in with two cups of chai. "Break time?" he asked, grinning.

"Always," Ankit replied, setting his laptop aside.

They sat on the terrace, sipping their chai in silence before Shubham spoke. "You know, failure sucks. No one prepares you for how much it hurts. But it's part of the process, man."

Ankit nodded, staring at the horizon. "I get that, but it's hard not to feel like a failure. Every rejection makes me question if I'm good enough."

Shubham's expression turned serious. "Look, you've read the Gita, right? It's all about focusing on the journey, not the results. Every 'no' is just pushing you closer to the 'yes' that's meant for you."

Ankit managed a faint smile. Shubham's words, though simple, carried weight.

The days that followed weren't easy. Ankit faced more rejections, each one testing his resolve. But this time, he approached them differently. Instead of spiraling into despair, he saw them as stepping stones. He returned to his notebook after each setback, reflecting on what he could improve and reminding himself of his worth.

He reconnected with classmates, joining group study sessions he had previously avoided. Slowly, he started rebuilding his confidence. The coding challenges he once dreaded became opportunities to learn and grow.

One afternoon, his mother called. This time, he answered. "Ma, I've been struggling," he admitted, his voice cracking.

"I know, beta," she replied gently. "But struggles make you stronger. We're proud of you, no matter what."

Her words brought tears to his eyes. For the first time in weeks, he felt a glimmer of hope.

As placement season continued, Shubham announced one evening that he had cleared the technical round for a prestigious multinational firm. "The final list is coming out tomorrow!" he exclaimed, his excitement contagious.

The next day, Ankit and Shubham walked to the notice board together. A small crowd had gathered, murmuring about the names on the list. Ankit scanned the sheet, his eyes landing on Shubham's name.

"You did it!" he said, clapping his friend on the back.

But then, his gaze moved further down—and froze. There it was: *Anishka Sharma.*

His heart skipped a beat. Memories flooded back, unbidden. The laughter, the arguments, the dreams they had once shared. Seeing her name stirred emotions he thought he had buried.

Shubham noticed his reaction. "She's just another name on the list now, bro," he said quietly. "Focus on your own path."

Ankit nodded, taking a deep breath. His fingers curled into a fist, then relaxed. The sight of her name hurt, but it didn't break him. For the first time, he felt the strength to let the past remain where it belonged.

"Healing isn't about forgetting the pain; it's about learning to live with it and letting it shape you into someone stronger. The journey isn't linear, but every step forward matters."

Chapter 21

Rebuilding the Future

The early morning sun cast a pale glow over the dormitory as Ankit's phone buzzed with a flurry of messages. The WhatsApp group was alive with activity, a cacophony of congratulations and chatter.

"Shubham, you did it, bro! 26 LPA! Insane!"

"Anishka nailed it too! 15 LPA offer! What a win!"

"Shubham, party toh banti hai!"

Ankit stared at the screen, his emotions swirling. Pride for Shubham's success swelled within him, but when his eyes landed on Anishka's name, a familiar ache resurfaced. Memories of late-night study sessions and whispered dreams came flooding back. She had moved on, thrived even. And here he was, struggling to find his footing.

As the group's excitement simmered, rumors began to bubble up.

"I heard Akash and his group helped Anishka prep for the coding rounds. She barely attended any sessions."

"Only two technical rounds? How'd she crack it?"

Ankit put his phone down, the whispers gnawing at him. His mind drifted to the countless hours he had spent teaching Anishka algorithms, debugging her projects, and guiding her through concepts she had struggled with. Despite it all, she had crossed him in the hallway earlier that week, her gaze fixed ahead as if he didn't exist.

That evening, Ankit sat on his bed, scrolling through the gallery on his phone. Each photo felt like a punch to the gut: Anishka laughing during a canteen break, holding a trophy from their hackathon, smiling candidly in a group photo. The moments they had shared, once a source of joy, now felt like cruel reminders.

He selected all the photos and hesitated, his thumb hovering over the delete button. Memories of their connection flashed before him—the time he stayed up all night helping her with a project, the promises they had made to support each other through placements.

With a deep breath, he pressed delete. The screen turned blank. A tear rolled down his cheek as the weight of letting go crashed over him.

Ravi found him in the common room later that night, his eyes red and puffy. "Ankit, kya hua? Why do you look so broken?"

Ankit's voice cracked as he spoke. "I taught her everything, Ravi. Five months—five months of projects, coding sessions, and late nights. I gave her everything I could. And now, she doesn't even acknowledge me."

Ravi sat beside him, his usual jovial expression replaced with concern. "Ankit, she's not worth it. You gave her your time and effort, and if she can't value that, it's her loss—not yours."

Shubham joined them, his tone firmer. "Bro, you're letting her control your emotions even now. She's moved on, and so should you. You've got so much potential—stop wasting it on someone who doesn't see it."

Ankit looked at his friends, their words cutting through his anguish. "It's not just her. It's everything. The placements, the rejections, the feeling of being left behind."

Shubham leaned in, his voice steady. "Failure doesn't define you, Ankit. It's how you rise after failure that matters. You've read the Gita, haven't you? Life isn't about the results—it's about giving your best."

As graduation approached, the atmosphere on campus grew tense. Most students had secured placements, leaving only a handful scrambling for opportunities. Even those who had struggled with coding had landed jobs through persistence or sheer luck. Ankit, once resolute about aiming high, now found himself lowering his expectations.

He applied for jobs offering 3 LPA, 4 LPA, even positions with bonds he had once sworn he'd never consider. Each rejection felt like a blow to his confidence, but the fear of graduating without a job overshadowed his pride.

One afternoon, he received a congratulatory message in the WhatsApp group:

"Congrats Ankit! Cleared the final round! 4 LPA offer!"

The words felt hollow. He had done it—secured a job—but the excitement was absent. The offer was far below what he had once dreamed of, and he couldn't help but feel like he had settled.

That evening, Ankit mustered the courage to call his parents. His mother picked up after the first ring. "Ankit! Kya hua, beta? You never call this late."

"I got a job, Ma," he said quietly.

Her voice lit up with joy. "That's wonderful, beta! Tell me everything!"

"It's 4 LPA," he admitted, his voice heavy with disappointment.

There was a pause before she replied, "And? That's still something to be proud of."

"But it's not what I wanted," Ankit confessed. "I thought I'd achieve more. I feel like I've let you and Papa down."

His father's steady voice joined the call, his tone comforting yet firm. "Ankit, life isn't about starting at the top. It's about perseverance. This is just the beginning. You've worked hard, and you've achieved something many people dream of. Don't undervalue that."

His mother added, "Beta, you're judging yourself too harshly. Do you know when your grandfather passed away, your father was left with nothing but debt? People mocked him, doubted him. But he worked tirelessly, built everything from scratch. Today, we have enough to support you because of his sacrifices."

Her voice cracked slightly as she continued, "And Ankit, remember this: no matter what happens, we'll always have your back. If you want to aim higher later, we'll support you. We're proud of you—not for the job, but for the person you've become."

Ankit felt a lump in his throat, tears streaming down his face. "Thank you, Ma, Papa. I'll make you proud."

After the call, Ankit sat at his desk, his parents' words echoing in his mind. He opened his copy of the Bhagavad Gita, flipping to a bookmarked page. One verse stood out:

"You have the right to perform your duty, but not to the fruits of your actions. Do not let the results of your work bind you."

He wrote the quote on a sticky note and pinned it to his wall. Beneath it, he added a line of his own:

"This is not the end—it's just the beginning."

The days that followed were not easy, but they were different. Ankit started seeing the 4 LPA offer not as a failure, but as a foundation. He began attending group study sessions again, reconnecting with his classmates, and even helping juniors prepare for their placements.

His website, which had once been a personal project to showcase his skills, now became a space for reflection. He shared his journey—the highs, the lows, the lessons he had learned. It became a source of motivation not just for him, but for others.

One evening, as Shubham and Ravi sat in their room, Ankit joined them with a quiet smile. "You know," he said, "I'm not where I thought I'd be. But I'm okay with that. I'll keep working, keep improving. This isn't the end."

Shubham grinned, clapping him on the back. "That's the spirit, bro. You've got this."

As the final four weeks of college approached, Ankit felt a renewed sense of purpose. He wasn't just surviving anymore—he was rebuilding, one step at a time.

"Sometimes, the greatest victories are not in what we achieve, but in how we choose to keep moving forward."

Chapter 22

The Turning Point

6 months Later........

The grand event hall was a sight to behold. Rows of neatly arranged chairs stretched out, filled with students, professors, and proud parents. The walls were adorned with the college banner, declaring **"Graduation and Achievement Ceremony: Celebrating Excellence"** in bold, glittering letters. On the stage sat six seats, each marked with nameplates of the top achievers. Beside each chair was a small table holding a bottle of water and a microphone, ready for the speakers to share their stories.

The college had gone all out for this event. A large LED screen at the back of the stage displayed the college logo, while cameras streamed the ceremony live on YouTube and Facebook for all students and alumni to watch. The air buzzed with anticipation as everyone took their seats.

A voice crackled through the microphone, silencing the murmurs in the hall. "Ladies and gentlemen, we are about to begin. Please maintain decorum as we welcome our esteemed guests and celebrate the achievements of our outstanding students."

The announcer, a polished woman in a crisp saree, took the stage. Her voice was clear and commanding. "Welcome to the annual Graduation and Achievement Ceremony of our college. Today, we honor not just academic excellence but also the spirit of resilience, determination, and transformation. Let's celebrate those who have not only excelled but also inspired."

The first name was called. "Please welcome Akash Verma, the topper of our final year, with a placement of 32 LPA at Google India." Applause filled the hall as Akash walked confidently to the stage, taking his seat with a proud smile.

The announcer continued. "Next, we have Shubham Sharma, who secured an incredible offer of 26 LPA from a leading multinational company." Shubham received a thunderous round of applause, his parents beaming from the front row.

"Shruti Iyer, an exceptional performer, with an offer of 22 LPA, is our third guest on stage today." Shruti, graceful and composed, joined the others.

The atmosphere grew electric as the announcer paused, building suspense. "And now, for a name that has made history. This student didn't just rise above challenges but shattered expectations. He started with the lowest on-campus placement but achieved a record-breaking international offer of **80 LPA off-campus**. Ladies and gentlemen, please welcome... **Ankit Tiwari**!"

The hall erupted in cheers. Parents clapped enthusiastically, students whistled and hollered, and the cameras panned to Ankit, who sat in the audience. He hesitated for a moment, then stood, straightened his blazer, and walked toward the stage. Each step felt surreal, the applause wrapping around him like a warm embrace. He caught Shubham's grin as he took his seat, feeling a surge of gratitude for the journey that had brought him here.

The audience buzzed with anticipation as Shubham stood up to address the crowd. Adjusting the microphone, he looked out at the sea of faces—students, parents, professors, and his closest friends. Taking a deep breath, he began, his voice warm and steady.

"Good afternoon, everyone. First of all, I'd like to thank our college and the organizers for giving us this platform to share our stories. But today, I don't want to talk too much about myself. My journey has been great, but it pales in comparison to someone who I believe is the true inspiration for this batch and the ones to come."

He glanced toward Ankit, who sat in the spotlight, looking slightly uncomfortable but smiling faintly. The crowd, sensing a story worth listening to, quieted down further.

"I want to talk about my friend, Ankit Tiwari. If there's one name that should motivate you—especially those who are struggling with placements, self-doubt, or failures—it's his."

Shubham's tone grew more reflective as he continued. "You see, when we started this placement journey, Ankit wasn't the strongest candidate. In fact, there was a time when he doubted himself so much that he almost gave up. I saw him fail coding tests. I saw him cry after rejections. I saw him struggle with emotions that would've crushed anyone else. But here's what makes Ankit different: he didn't let those failures define him. Instead, he used them to rebuild himself."

The audience listened intently as Shubham's voice filled with admiration. "In the last eight months, I've watched him change completely. He turned his pain into purpose. He didn't just prepare for interviews—he prepared for life. Ankit became relentless, but not in an aggressive way. He found balance through spirituality, especially in the teachings of the **Bhagavad Gita**."

Shubham paused for a moment, letting his words sink in. "Let me tell you something about Ankit's journey. He started small—analyzing every failure, writing down every mistake he made in a notebook, and working tirelessly to improve. He didn't let rejection discourage him. Instead, he saw every 'no' as a stepping stone to the eventual 'yes.' He made consistency his mantra, and he stuck to it."

Shubham smiled. "But it wasn't just about coding or placements. Ankit worked on himself as a person. He let go of the negativity that was holding him back, be it self-doubt or the emotional baggage of past relationships. He stopped blaming circumstances and started taking control of his life."

Shubham's voice softened, and a smile played on his lips. "I don't want to get too emotional, but seeing Ankit up here today makes me proud. He's not just my friend—he's my inspiration. And I know he's an inspiration to many of you sitting here."

The audience clapped softly, sensing the genuine bond between the two friends.

Shubham chuckled, breaking the somber mood. "But before I turn this into a TED Talk, let me just say one last thing: if you're ever in doubt, just remember Ankit's journey. And now, I'm going to do something I know Ankit hates—put him on the spot. Ankit, my friend, it's time for you to share your story. The stage is yours."

The audience broke into applause as Shubham stepped back, gesturing for Ankit to take the mic. Ankit, though still shy, stood up with newfound confidence. The spotlight shifted to him, and the room grew quiet as everyone leaned in to hear the words of the student who had overcome the odds.

The stage was set, not just for Ankit's speech, but for the culmination of a journey that would inspire everyone present.

Ankit stood, his heart pounding. Public speaking wasn't his strength, but today felt different. He took the microphone, glancing briefly at the audience before speaking.

"Good afternoon, everyone. To be honest, I never imagined myself standing here. Eight months ago, I was lost—lost in failures, self-doubt, and emotions I didn't know how to handle. I made mistakes, a lot of them. But I learned something important: mistakes don't define you. What defines you is how you respond to them."

He paused, the room hanging on his every word.

"I want to thank my parents for their unconditional support. Ma, Papa—your belief in me kept me going. To my friends, Shubham and Ravi, thank you for never letting me give up. And to Krishna and Hanuman Ji, and the teachings of the **Bhagavad Gita**, I owe my transformation to the wisdom I found there."

Ankit's voice grew steadier. "To everyone here: if you make mistakes, don't let them become a disease that eats away at your confidence. Even cancer can be treated with determination. Fight with your mind, control your emotions, and trust the process."

He ended with a quote from the **Gita**:

"The mind is restless and difficult to restrain, but it can be conquered through practice and detachment."

The hall fell silent for a moment before erupting into a standing ovation. Ankit stepped back, overwhelmed by the applause, as students, parents, and professors rose to their feet.

As the event concluded, certificates were distributed. Students mingled, taking photos with friends and family. Ankit stood with Shubham and Ravi, laughing about their journey, when he noticed someone walking toward him.

It was Anishka.

"Congratulations, Ankit," she said softly. "And... I'm sorry. For everything."

As he walked away, a wave of emotions washed over Ankit. He felt a pang of sadness, remembering the bond they once shared. But there was also a sense of relief, a lightness he hadn't felt in months. He had finally let go. Anishka's apology, though belated, was enough. It wasn't about forgiveness or blame anymore; it was about accepting that chapter of his life was over and embracing the future.

Two years later, Ankit sat at his desk in his Bengaluru apartment, overlooking the bustling city. His laptop screen glowed with lines of code, a testament to his successful career as a software developer. He had come a long way from the heartbroken young man who had once felt lost and alone. He had found his passion, built a fulfilling life, and even reconnected with his love for cricket, joining a local club on weekends. As he glanced at a framed photo of him with Shubham and Ravi, a wave of gratitude washed over him. He had learned that life wasn't about avoiding setbacks, but about rising above them, stronger and wiser.

"In the journey of life, it's not the setbacks that define you, but the courage to rise, rebuild, and move forward. Success isn't just about achieving goals—it's about becoming the person you were meant to be."

"The First Steps"

(The struggles, insecurities, and the beginning of Ankit's college life)

In halls adorned with endless dreams,
Lie whispers faint and self-doubt screams.
A lecture starts, a test unfolds,
The weight of future tightly holds.

Lost in books and a sea of peers,
Each failure echoes, feeds the fears.
Rejections sting, and silence looms,
Nights dissolve in quiet rooms.

Yet hope appears, a fragile flame,
In friends who call you by your name.
With chai and jokes, the walls come down,
In laughter shared, the lost are found.

The Bhagavad Gita's wisdom seeps,
Through restless minds and sleepless weeks.
It whispers, "Detach, find your way,
For effort shines when doubts betray."

~ By Amitesh Mani Tiwari

"The Ties That Bind"

(Friendships, love, and the emotional journey of college life)

In crowded halls, where dreams collide,
Friendships bloom, like rivers wide.
Ravi's jokes and Shubham's plan,
Together they form a solid clan.

Anishka's smile, a fleeting light,
Brought warmth by day and storms by night.
She taught him love, she taught him pain,
Through her, he grew, though heartbreak came.

Nights of tears and silent screams,
Felt heavier than broken dreams.
But in the cracks, the light broke through,
With every fall, a lesson grew.

For love may falter, and paths may part,
Yet memories linger, etched in the heart.
Through bonds of steel, unspoken ties,
The spirit of college forever flies.

~ By Amitesh Mani Tiwari

"The Turning Point"

(A reflection of college life and its transformative journey)

We entered these gates, unsure and small,
The world seemed vast, and we knew so little at all.
In crowded halls and lecture rooms,
We faced our fears and embraced the unknown's gloom.

Sleepless nights with deadlines near,
Dreams entangled with doubt and fear.
Yet, in every stumble, in every fall,
We learned to rise and stand tall.

Friendships formed in the mess and the dorm,
Through chai breaks and banter, we weathered the storm.
Jokes that lingered, bonds that grew,
Moments that healed and carried us through.

There were highs of triumph, lows of defeat,
In the race for placements, the heart skipped a beat.
But failure taught us, not how to quit,
But to find our strength and commit.

We found wisdom in verses old,
The Gita's truth, its lessons bold:
Detach from fear, let go of shame,
True success lies in playing the game.

The stage arrived, the spotlight's call,
Our names echoed in the grand hall.
Certificates clutched with pride and tears,
A chapter closing, yet one that endears.

Now, as we look back, the lessons are clear,
It wasn't just grades that brought us here.
It was resilience born from the trials we faced,
And the bonds we formed in this sacred space.

"College isn't just a phase we survive,
It's the place where we truly come alive.
The turning point, where dreams take flight,
A beacon that shines through life's darkest night."

~ By Amitesh Mani Tiwari

www.ingramcontent.com/pod-product-compliance
Lightning Source LLC
LaVergne TN
LVHW042343150826
845671LV00001B/4

* 9 7 9 8 8 9 6 7 3 8 4 3 5 *